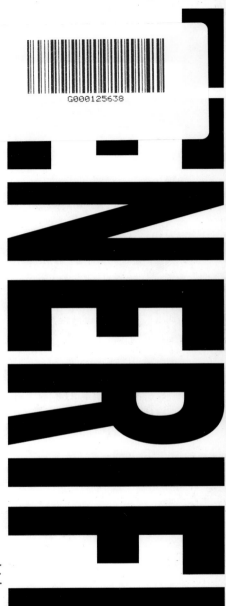

TENERIFE

& LA GOMERA

SPIRALGUIDE

AA Publishing

G000125638

Contents

Written by Damien Simonis
Listings sections written by Lindsay Hunt
Revised and updated by Lindsay Bennett

Project Editor Claire Strange
Project Designer Alison Fenton
Series Editor Karen Rigden
Series Designer Catherine Murray

Published by AA Publishing, a trading name of AA Media Limited,
whose registered office is Fanum House, Basing View, Basingstoke,
Hampshire, RG21 4EA. Registered number 06112600.

ISBN: 978-0-7495-6248-9

The contents of this publication are believed correct at the time
of printing. Nevertheless, AA Publishing accept no responsibility
for errors, omissions or changes in the details given, or for the
consequences of reader's reliance on this information. This does
not affect your statutory rights. Assessments of attractions, hotels,
restaurants and so forth are based on the author's own experience
and contain subjective opinions that may not reflect the publisher's
opinion or a reader's experience. We have tried to ensure accuracy in
this guide, but things do change, so please let us know if you have any
comments or corrections.

A CIP catalogue record for this book is available from the
British Library.

Cover design and binding by permission of AA Publishing
Colour separation by Keenes, Andover
Printed and bound in China by Leo Paper Products

Find out more about AA Publishing and the wide range of travel
publications and services the AA provides by visiting our website at
www.theAA.com/bookshop

A03805
Maps in this title produced from mapping © KOMPASS GmbH,
A-6063 Rum/Innsbruck

The Magazine

A great holiday is more than just lying on a beach or shopping till you drop — to really get the most from your trip you need to know what makes the place tick. The Magazine provides an entertaining overview to some of the social, cultural and natural elements that make up the unique character of this engaging island.

ISLAND LIFE

On first impressions you might think that Tenerife is a chunk of Britain teleported to the sunshine. English breakfasts and Sunday roasts, plus Premier League football shown in sports bars are typical of Playa des las Americas and Los Cristianos.

Perhaps it's not surprising; Of the almost 3.4 million non-Spanish tourists who took holidays on the island in 2007, almost half (1.5 million) were British (twice as many as the next nearest nationality – the Germans). Twenty thousand Brits live here year-round, with double that number owning holiday or second homes.

More Than Just a Tourist Enclave

It would be easy to assume that Tenerife was rolling over and giving itself up to this invasion of foreigners, but Tenerife is still very much a Canarian island with a robust culture.

Universidad de la Laguna is an obvious and vigorous counterbalance to euro-vacation land. The 25,000 students arriving from all across the country represent a contemporary and energetic 21st-century Spanish

The beach at Playa de Las Teresitas is an artificial marvel

influence on the island. And Santa Cruz de Tenerife is an authentic
Spanish city; this is one of Spain's most exciting cityscapes, and a perfect
place for that most traditional of Spanish pastimes, the evening *paseo*.

Did You Know?

Morocco and Spain are in a longstanding stand-off about who should have
territorial rights over the Canaries. Since there are signs of oil reserves in
the offshore seabed around the islands this may be about more than just
the rocks. In 2002 Morocco rejected the latest Spanish proposal to end
the dispute, but don't expect the row to escalate beyond a war of words.

TENERIFE FACTS

- Tenerife is one of eight islands that make up the archipelago of the Islas
  Canarias or Canary Islands.
- The autonomous region is made up of two provinces – Santa Cruz de
  Tenerife (incorporating Tenerife, La Palma, La Gomera and El Hierro) and
  Las Palmas (incorporating Gran Canaria, Fuerteventura and Lanzarote).
- The Canary Islands have thirteen seats in the Spanish Senate (government)
  plus two elected by the autonomous council. Tenerife supplies three seats.
- The Canary Islands make up 4.5 per cent of the total Spanish population.
  They have an average population density of 268 people per square
  kilometre, but Tenerife's is higher with a population density of 419 people
  per square kilometre.

CARNAVAL
AND OTHER FESTIVALS

Tenerife's calendar bursts with fiestas of all sorts, ranging from noisy town processions to *romerías*, festive pilgrimages from a town's central church into the country, often ending at a beautifully remote rural chapel.

Often the townspeople get together in traditional dress and treat the whole thing as much like a mobile party as a religious experience. Religious celebrations and saints' days are indeed the most common excuse for a fiesta. One exception is Carnaval (Carnival), whose roots go back to obscure pagan rituals greeting the imminent arrival of spring.

Santa Cruz Goes Mad

Carnaval is celebrated throughout Tenerife, but nowhere with the same determined madness as in the capital, Santa Cruz. Although the festivities go on for three weeks in February, the core events and spectacular parades of scantily clad dancers last for a week. Only the craziness of Rio de Janeiro outdoes the Tenerife show, which ends six weeks before Easter.

Each year the organisers choose a theme (in 2009, Monsters in literature and film). After the first few days of mask competitions, concerts, parades, children's events and heats for the election of the Carnival Queen *(Reina del Carnaval)*, the serious celebrations begin with the gala night for the election of the queen, usually on a Wednesday night.

> "Only the craziness of Rio de Janeiro outdoes the Tenerife show"

The following Friday the grand parade takes place and on the Wednesday after is the "burial of the sardine", when a procession takes a symbolic sardine around town for burial, marking the end of Carnaval and the countdown to the reawakening of spring. The long nights of dancing continue until the end of the following weekend.

Several other traditional festivities throughout the year are well worth a visit. In many cases specific dates change from year to year.

Carnaval Queen contestant Luz Yurena Martin performs in Santa Cruz de Tenerife

Local farmers with their cattle in the Fiesta Romería

May
Los Realejos: Romería de San Isidro Labrador

The earliest records referring to this festive pilgrimage date back to 1676. In those days farmers from around Los Realejos, on the outskirts of Puerto de la Cruz, would gather to lead ox-driven carts through the steep streets of town. Nowadays the gaily decorated carts are hauled around on the back of trucks after a ceremony in honour of San Isidro, the patron of farmers.

June
La Orotava: Octava de Corpus Cristi – Fiesta de las Alfombras

The citizens of La Orotava go to huge lengths to celebrate Corpus Cristi (the Thursday following the eighth Sunday after Easter). Apart from services and processions, the high point is the unveiling of remarkable carpets made from flower petals and volcanic sands. For days before the event, the town keeps busy designing the carpets and peeling petals from countless flowers to fill them in. The most spectacular of the carpets is made in the Plaza del Ayuntamiento. Tonnes of different coloured sands from the Circo de las Cañadas mountain chain in the Teide National Park (► 118) are used to compose a Biblical triptych in the square.

June
La Orotava: Romería de San Isidro Labrador y Santa María de la Cabeza

The Sunday after Corpus Cristi (► above), La Orotava takes to the streets for this colourful parade. As in Los Realejos, there has been a centuries-old tradition among local farmers of celebrating a Romería de San Isidro. Today the festivities retain all the appearance of a country affair, with cow-drawn carts and farmers dressed as magicians.

July
La Laguna: Romería de San Benito Abad

This procession features seven women representing the seven islands of the archipelago. Followed by a colourful array of people, floats, carts, dancing around maypoles and general noisy chaos, they liven up the decorated streets of La Laguna for a day.

15 August
Candelaria: Fiesta de Nuestra Señora de la Candelaria (Assumption)

Though the official feast day of Nuestra Señora de la Candelaria is 2 February, it has long been celebrated in August too. Pilgrims converge on foot on Candelaria and on 14 August a grand ceremony takes place in Plaza de la Basílica to commemorate the legendary apparition of the miraculous statue of the Virgin Mary to the Guanches (► 128). This is followed by a procession to the nearby Pozo de la Virgen (Virgin's Well), where fireworks are lit. On 15 August a big Mass is held in front of the basilica, with another noisy procession.

August
Garachico: Romería de San Roque

When plague struck Garachico and the surrounding area in the 17th century, the people appealed for help from the saint of plague victims, the 14th-century French St Roch, revered for having devoted himself to bringing succour to plague victims in Italy and southern France. Centuries later, the people of Garachico still converge once a year on the rural chapel of San Roque, outside Garachico, to transport an image of the saint to the Iglesia de Santa Ana in Garachico, where Mass is celebrated. Then the people of the town and farmers, accompanied by bands, carts and flocks of farm animals, engage in a procession to take San Roque back to his chapel.

30 November
Puerto de la Cruz and Icod de los Vinos: Festividad de San Andrés

No one has worked out what St Andrew has to do with drinking, but on the eve of his feast day the *bodegas* (wine cellars) of Tenerife throw open their doors to ring in the year's new wines. In some towns, like Puerto de la Cruz (► 93) and Icod de los Vinos (► 96), they celebrate in a loud manner, with chaotic parades.

Traditional dress is often worn at fiestas

The land of the
Guanches

In May 1493, a Spanish force of 1,000 infantry and 150 horses landed on Tenerife near present-day Santa Cruz. Led by Alonso Fernández de Lugo, their mission was to conquer the last of the seven Canary Islands.

A painting representing the Guanches is on display in the Santa Cruz townhall

The other six had been taken since 1402 in an intermittent campaign run by mercenaries, freebooters and other misfits for the Spanish crown.

The story of the island's conquest had so far been a predictably sad tale of trickery, massacre, enslavement and exile with the Spaniards being remarkably ineffectual on occasion in the face of the bows and arrows and guerrilla tactics of the islanders.

Earlier landings on Tenerife had proven fruitless, but the Europeans had been able to hang around long enough to cast an eye over the locals, by whom they were clearly impressed. Reports described them as tall, blond and blue-eyed. They called themselves Guanches, from *guan* (man) and *che*, a word that referred to Mount Teide. The Guanches were thus the "People of Teide" (or by extension of Tenerife). Subsequently the name Guanche came to be applied to the natives of all the islands, although they were divided into many different tribes.

Who Were the Guanches?

Who were the Guanches and where did they come from? The clues are sparse. Carbon-dating of archaeological finds suggests the islands were inhabited from at least 200 BC. It appears most likely that the islanders' ancestors migrated from North Africa, a mere 100km (62 miles) east. The people of the easternmost islands, Lanzarote and Fuerteventura, were almost definitely descendants of Berber tribes. Various theories suggest that the blond hair and blue eyes came from ancient Basque migrants or adventurous Norse raiders.

The Guanches led a primitive Stone-Age existence, mostly living in caves and subsisting by a combination of hunting, herding and simple farming. The main sources of food were goats and fish. Barley was ground and toasted to form *gofio*, a basic staple still eaten today. Tools and weapons were made of wood, stone and bone. Simple dugouts were used to skirt the coast and, on occasion, to travel to the other islands.

First Contact

The first European contact with the Guanches probably came in the late 13th century. One missionary expedition is recorded in 1341, although earlier contacts had probably been made before by fortune-hunters looking for the Atlantic outlet of the fabled African Río de Oro (Gold River), along which huge quantities of the precious metal were supposedly transported.

Guanche Downfall

The nine separate fiefs on Tenerife were each ruled by a *mencey* (chief). The feuds between the nine tribes proved to be the Guanches' undoing. It seems unlikely they had not heard of the disasters that had befallen their cousins on the other islands, and yet at least two *menceys* sided with the invaders. The Spaniards' most implacable adversary was *mencey* Bencomo, backed by three others. In spring 1494 de Lugo launched his first armed attack, an unmitigated disaster, and it was more than two years before the Guanches surrendered – weakened more by a mysterious epidemic than cowed by Spanish arms.

In the following decades some Guanches, living in the more remote parts of the island, continued low-level guerrilla resistance, but within a century they had been brought to heel. A few generations after the conquest they had largely assimilated with their conquerors. All that remains today are many curious place names.

Statue of a Guanche chief in Candelaria

FREAKY FLOWERS

In spite of the wholesale felling of forests over the centuries and the rapid spread of urban and tourist development across the island, Tenerife can still claim to be extraordinarily rich in flora, with some 1,400 species of plants.

This passion flower may not be native to the Canaries but it thrives in the climate

This is, in part, a result of the climate, for the island is said to enjoy as many as 50 distinct microclimates. No fewer than 140 species are endemic to the island, and about 200 to the archipelago. Come in late winter and early spring and you can see the native plants and trees of Tenerife at their vivacious colourful best.

Trees
Among the trees, the dragon tree *(drago)* is emblematic. It is an odd beast. From a long smooth trunk, branches poke out at the top like fat sausages from which long, scary-looking leaves stand on end.

Another important tree is the laurel, found in parts of northeast Tenerife and in the Garajonay National Park on La Gomera (➤ 150). Often covered in lichen and enveloped in mist, these laurel woods are about all that remain of pre-Ice-Age forests. It is hard to imagine that millions of years ago much of the Mediterranean was covered in extensive laurel forests like these. More common than either the dragon or the laurel is the Canary pine, whose lumber goes into many of the balconies, doors and window frames in traditional island housing.

Flowers

Next to the dragon tree, the best-known floral symbol is the blood red *tajinaste rojo* (Teide Vipers Bugloss). It is found at altitudes of 2,000– 2,500m (6,560–8,200 feet) near Mount Teide. Its long, upright spike covered in little red flowers is instantly recognisable (mid-spring to early summer). Other flowers that flourish in the Teide National Park (▶ 118) include the Teide straw, with yellow flowers, and the pink Teide scabious.

An odd plant you may mistakenly take for a kind of cactus is the curious *cardón* (candelabra spurge). Clusters of slender, pale-green, tube-like stems grow up to 3m (10-feet) high and are covered in short spikes. It is most common in semi-arid locations.

Look also for the Canary orchid, with its pink blossoms in winter. Another winter bloomer is the lovely Canary bell-flower, with reddish-orange flowers. Various ferns flourish in the laurel forests and many other varieties of plants and flowers grow in different parts of the island.

Strelitzia are commonly known as Bird of Paradise flowers

PIRATES, PRIVATEERS AND A BAD DAY FOR
LORD NELSON

On 30 April, 1657, Admiral Robert Blake appeared with a fleet of 33 warships off the coast of Santa Cruz. Spain and England were at war, and Blake was ordered to capture a bullion fleet due to anchor in the town's port.

From the earliest days of the *Conquista* of Latin America, the English had taken an interest in the fleets that poured America's mineral wealth into Spain's coffers. In 1572, Queen Elizabeth I awarded Sir Francis Drake a commission as a privateer. England backed Protestant Holland in its rebellion against Catholic Spain and Drake relished the chance to avenge some rough treatment he had received four years earlier from the Spaniards in the Caribbean. This he set about doing with some success, raiding bullion ships all over the Atlantic and several times threatening the Canary Islands, the Spanish ships' main port of call.

Privateer or Pirate?

As far as Madrid was concerned Drake and Blake were pirates. As Blake's fleet closed on Santa Cruz, the town opened fire. The English and Spanish versions of the outcome differ. Blake claimed to have sent the bulk of the Spanish ships to the bottom of the sea, but Madrid declared a victory, with 200 English seamen killed or wounded, and only five Spanish casualties. Santa Cruz even added a lion to its coat-of-arms as a pat on the back. In November 1706 the English were back, this time with Admiral Jennings as their leader, who, with 13 warships, attempted a landing at Santa Cruz. He was forced to withdraw and Santa Cruz got another lion.

Richard Westall's painting of Nelson being wounded at Santa Cruz in 1797

(H)armless?

The city crest was to receive one further lion. The young Rear Admiral Horatio Nelson was on patrol in the Mediterranean in early 1797 when he was instructed to seize Santa Cruz. With a squadron of eight vessels he arrived on 22 July. Two days later he landed his troops, but after just one night it was clear he had failed, despite the might of more than 390 cannon fired on the land batteries by his ships. The bitterness of failure was compounded by a grapeshot wound to his right arm, which surgeons were obliged to amputate.

> "the British weighed anchor and quietly slipped away"

The Spaniards were exultant but gracious. British wounded were treated and returned to their ships, although their captured ensigns (still in the Museo Militar in Santa Cruz, ➤ 59) were not. On 26 July, the British weighed anchor and quietly slipped away.

English warships in action at Santa Cruz

Get Active!

Bored with lazing around on the beach? Tenerife has plenty of distractions if you want to get active. It's a great place to try a new sport or two and has some pretty unusual traditional pastimes that you may want to sit out!

Sports Fishing

Tenerife's position on the edge of the deep ocean trenches attracts an amazing array of species that keeps even the most avid sports fisherman happy. Billfish are the biggest and most prized game catches: These large fast predatory species are top of the ocean food chain. Atlantic Blue Marlin can reach 7m (23 feet) in length, weigh in at 450kg/1000lbs and swim at 80kph/50mph. Other billfish species found off Tenerife include White Marlin and sailfish, plus there's also a chance of hooking a Mako Shark. But none of these species is for eating. If you fish for your supper, you'll probably end up with a hold full of bonito (a member of the mackerel family); dorado (also called the dolphin fish or mahi-mahi), and wahoo. Big Game Fishing Charters, tel: 922/736-759; www.biggamefishingcharters.com

Kitesurfing

This high-energy and high-adrenalin sport has exploded on the scene in the last decade and the vast coastal offshore shallows at El Médano in the southeast of Tenerife offer ideal conditions. The trade winds can almost be guaranteed here, and the waters are divided into zones with a range of sea and wind conditions. It's attracted current professional riders like Steve Verelst to spend their training time here. Ex-kitesurfing world champion

Windsurfing conditions around the islands are excellent

Arona's golf course is inland from Playa de las Américas

Mark Shinn was so impressed with conditions on Tenerife that he opened a training centre here in 2006 that's now one of the best in the business. The Shinn Centre, tel: 922/179-401, www.theshinncentre.com

Golf

Year-round sunshine and warm temperatures are ideal conditions for golf. Tenerife has a choice of eight courses. José "Pepe" Gancedo, a successful amateur golfer – six times Spanish champion – has built a solid reputation as a course designer. Christened the "Picasso of golf course design" for his avant-garde ideas, he is architect of the Golf des Sur and the Costa Adeje courses. Seve Ballesteros had a much higher profile as a player – five major tournaments in a playing career stretching from 1974 to 1995 – but he's turned his hand to design, stamping his mark on Buenavista Golf.

Weird Wrestling

The island's inhabitants, the Guanches, were keen warriors. To keep fit, the men sparred in bouts of strength and skill, a form of which has survived to this day. Known as *lucha canaria* (Canarian wrestling), it has a popular following. Teams of up to 12 wrestlers compete in tag-team wrestling: a cross between Greco-Roman and sumo wrestling. The key rule is that no part of the body but the soles of the feet may touch the ground. The first to break this rule loses. To find out where to see matches, contact the Federación de Lucha Canaria, Calle Maya 3, La Laguna, tel: 922/251-452; www.federaciondeluchacanaria.com

Juego del Palo

The Guanches had several variants of the *juego del palo* ("stick game") including one where, armed with heavy staffs and stones, tribal opponents attempted to smash each other's bones. A modern version you might see at fiestas is more a trial of skill using 2m (6.5-foot) long poles.

Here there be
WHALES

Tenerife is one of the best places in the world to go whale watching – whatever the time of year. A huge array of marine species funnel past the islands or prefer to live permanently in the fertile waters.

Pilot Whales are the most common species that you are likely to see. A large family pod has settled permanently around southern Tenerife; sightings of mothers and babies or nursery groups are a regular occurrence and particularly heart-lifting. Just as exciting are Bottlenose Dolphin encounters. These sociable creatures often dive in and out of the bow wake as boats travel along. There's a large population living year-round off Los Gigantes, though there are also regular sightings of groups of smaller, faster, Spotted Dolphin, and Stripped Dolphin.

Whale-watching opportunities are available all year round

However, you may be lucky enough to spot something more rare. Migratory species pass through heading north in the spring to feeding grounds in polar waters, returning south in the autumn, and more than 25 species of the order *Cetacea* (the group that encompasses whales, dolphins and porpoises) have been noted in the waters around Tenerife, including Sperm Whales and Right Whales. That's almost one third of all whale and dolphin species.

Watch and Learn

Most whale-watching operations have bases along the southern coast from harbours at Los Gigantes and marinas along the Costa Adeje (p125). Trips last around two hours and may include lunch or snacks onboard. However, one organisation offering these trips differs from the rest. The Atlantic Whale Foundation (www.whalenation.org) not only puts you close to the action, but it's also one of the most important charities working in the area of marine conservation.

If We Could Talk to the Animals – It's Incredible...

The D Nome Project is using musical sounds to try to communicate with the dolphins off Los Gigantes. Research aims to build a database of Dolphin sounds and behaviours to help with future conservation. The information will also be used to enhance programmes for human sufferers of conditions, such as autism, which are known to be improved by interaction with dolphins.

Tenerife's
EXPLOSIVE HISTORY

Leaving aside fanciful ideas that the Canary Islands are all that remain of the Lost Continent of Atlantis, it appears almost certain that they are a volcanic creation, although theories about just how they were created are many.

Modern science has divided the surface of the world into a series of tectonic plates, each interlocking and tending to pull away or crush into one another. One theory suggests the Canary Islands chain was thrown up in a weak area of the Earth's crust as a result of movement between the African and American continental plates, possibly 20 million years ago, in the Miocene Age.

Recent Eruptions
All the Canary Islands are volcanic, but none quite as spectacular as Tenerife. The last major eruption was in 1798 (a smaller one occurred in 1909), when a huge gash opened up along the southwestern flank of the Pico Viejo ("old peak") and spewed forth a barrage of molten magma.

Mount Teide

Although Mount Teide, the island's (and Spain's) highest mountain, attracts the most attention, it is just one of a series of volcanoes and fissures created along a fault line on the island millions of years ago. Mount Teide itself is a strato-volcano, a complex natural edifice that has been built up over the millennia.

Strato-volcanoes are created by repeated eruptions giving off lava flows and shooting volcanic material, known as pyroclasts, into the air. Each eruption adds another layer and so helps build up the cone. In such volcanoes cooling magma sometimes forms a "plug" right inside the cone. In a later eruption the plug acts like a lid on a pressure cooker – when it finally blows, the explosion frequently takes much of the cone with it.

Young Mountains

Mount Teide and its companion peaks are fairly new on the scene. It is estimated that the oldest volcanic rock formations still extant on the island go back seven million years, and include the Teno Massif in the northwest (► 163–164) and the Anaga mountain range in the northeast (► 73).

Three million years ago the bulk of the activity moved to the centre, apparently creating a huge volcano. The semicircular Circo de las Cañadas mountain chain south of Mount Teide is what remains of its ancient crater, inside which Mount Teide and its companions grew during later eruptions in the past 500,000 years.

Mount Teide has spectacular scenery

Los Roques de Garcia is within the Parque Nacional del Teide

This kind of massive crater, formed by the destruction of its cone, is called a caldera, and the caldera inside which Mount Teide grew is one of the biggest in the world. At 3,718m (12,195 feet), Mount Teide is right up there with Vesuvius, Kilimanjaro, Fujiyama and Etna. Compared with the millions of years of volcanic history on Tenerife, it is a relative newcomer, with a maximum of only half a million years on the clock.

Frozen Rivers
Volcanoes erupt in two main ways. In the first, magma (molten material from the Earth's mantle to a maximum depth of 600km/372 miles) boils up inside a single chimney, or vent. When the pressure finally forces an explosion, the magma spews up and meets the air at temperatures of anything from 700 to 1,200ºC (1,292 to 2,192ºF).

> "in 1798…a huge gash opened up along the southwestern flank of the Pico Viejo"

How far it flows down the mountain side before cooling depends largely on its material make up and viscosity. Masses of more treacle-like magma flows out of the cone, or fissures, further down the mountainside and flow downhill, slowing only as they cool and harden.

Around the slopes of Mount Teide you will see such "frozen" rivers, some of them reaching down to the road that crosses the park.

Volcanic Fissures

In the second, fissured, version of a volcanic eruption, cracks open further down the mountain and the magma is forced along a subsidiary pipe from the main chimney. Mount Teide shows evidence of both types of eruption. Gases dominate volcanic eruptions. They are the first element to reach the surface and consist mainly of water vapour. Gases exiting at great speed can break up the molten rock on its way to the top and send it shooting up into the air. The resulting fragments are pyroclasts.

Moonscape

The weird landscape around Mount Teide is dominated by basalt. But you can also see fragments of obsidian, which look like black glass. Scoria, high in magnesium and iron, is easily recognised by its reddish tinge. Tenerife is still volcanically active, as can be testified by the fumarolas, gaseous vapour rising from points around the peak. Mount Teide could yet again reveal its uniquely devilish side.

Volcanic landscape typical of Tenerife's high country

THE WIND OF CHANGE

Music for the Future

Eólica is the island's biggest music festival and it's claimed to be the world's first and only carbon-neutral festival. For two days and nights in July the summer air of southern Tenerife is filled with hot sounds that don't cost the Earth.

This must be one of the most dramatic impromptu festival venues on the planet. The sound stages are set in the lee of fields of the massive wind turbines (*eólicos* in Spanish) of the Instituto Tecnológico de Energías Renovables (Technical Institute for Renewable Energies, also known as ITER), one of Europe's leading research centres on sustainable power sources, and Spain's original Bioclimatic Park. ITER supplies all the electricity for the festival through its wind and solar power generation plants so no fossil fuels are burned and no CO_2 is released into the atmosphere.

Though some of the attendant stalls are rented by conservation-minded organisations, Eólica (www.eolica.es) isn't in the business of pushing the environment down anyone's throat. It's about having a great time and enjoying great music. The clips posted by festival-goers on You Tube will

give you a real feel for the atmosphere. The artistic aim is wide-ranging, with mainstream acts supported by an eclectic mix ranging from dance and circus artists to multimedia electronic screenings. In 2008 more than 40 artists performed, including Mercury-nominated UK band Asian Dub Foundation; El Columpio Asesino, a rock/punk style band from Pamplona; and Juliette and the Licks, an American indie-rock band fronted by actress Juliette Lewis. Eólica is fast becoming a hot gig on the global DJ circuit. Local favourite

"Eólica…is about having a great time and enjoying great music"

Alberto "Beto" Uña; DJonston, resident at Barcelona's BeCool club; British DJ Jim Rivers; and American remix artists Masters at Work and Ursula 1000 have all played sets.

The Instituto Tecnológico de Energías Renovables (ITER)

ITER's research could change all our lives. Scientists are helping to make wind energy more efficient and photovoltaic solar energy affordable, and they're exploring ideas that may lead us in new, as yet untried, directions for energy production as the century unfolds. The Solten I plant – currently ITER's largest – can supply the power needs of 5,300 families, saving over 1,000 tonnes per year in fossil fuels and keeping 18,000 tonnes per year of CO_2 out of the atmosphere.

The wind turbines at Punta de Teno

AFTER SUNSET...

Hot days on the beaches are followed by hot nights in the resorts of Playa de las Américas and Los Cristianos.

Playa de las Américas has the island's liveliest nightlife

The coastline around Playa de las Américas and Los Cristianos acts as a Mecca for young Europeans, for whom partying is the name of the game.

The Tenerife scene isn't hard-core clubbing like you'd find in Ibiza. Here the non-stop "free shot" and "two for one" offers lure the drinking crowd – offers backed by sports coverage from football (soccer) leagues around Europe. Later these same venues transform themselves into discos and clubs, with DJs performing till the early hours.

Bars in the south congregate around two famous "strips", Veronica's in Playa de las Américas and The Patch in Los Cristianos.

FOLLOW THE NOISE TO THE SCENE OF YOUR CHOICE

- Enjoy the *craic* (Gaelic for good times) at Irish bars Shenanigans, O'Neills, Dubliners or Gaelic Corner Bar.
- Try a place with a real English connection like Blaydon Races, The Full Monty or Lineker's, owned by the ex-footballer and now television presenter Gary Lineker and his family.
- Or look out for a nod to your holiday heaven at Pleasure Island, Oasis and American Dream.
- Liquid Club at Playa de las Américas is Tenerife's super-club. The sensuous curves of the psychedelic interior were designed by award-winning Spanish interior designer Tomás Alia.
- Joy in Santa Cruz is the capital's long-time favourite – where the action starts around 1am and continues till dawn.

Finding Your Feet

First Two Hours

Tenerife Sur (Reina Sofia) Airport

The bigger of the two airports on Tenerife, Tenerife Sur (Reina Sofia) is in the south, 20km (12.5 miles) east of Playa de las Américas.

- The airport takes almost all **international flights**, whether scheduled or charter (tel: 902/404-704).
- Up to **nine million** passengers pour through it every year.
- The airport **tourist information booth** (tel: 922/392-037) in the arrivals hall is open Oct–Apr Mon–Fri 9–9, Sat–Sun 9–5; May–Sep Mon–Fri 9–7, Sat–Sun 9–5.
- You can get **general information** on the island, as well as help with accommodation and public transport. They will point the way to buses, taxis and car-rental outlets in the airport.
- While you're here pick up a **map** of the island.

Transport from the Airport

Car Rental

- Car rental is **less expensive** compared to mainland Spain or many other European countries as the Canary Islands have special tax exemptions, which reduce the rate you pay.
- You can organise car rental **in advance** as part of your package or through most major international car-rental companies.
- To rent car you will need your **driver's licence** and must be at least 21 years old. Always have your licence, passport and car documentation with you.
- Generally you will need a **credit card** to rent a car.
- Before renting, **compare the cost of different companies**, taking into account insurance, collision damage waiver, extra passenger cover and IGIC (the local version of VAT).
- Most of the time you can get cars with **unlimited mileage** but do check the small print of the contract.
- A number of the major car-rental companies are represented at the airport near the arrivals hall. Many have offices elsewhere on Tenerife:
  Avis tel: 922/392-056; www.avis.com
  Europcar tel: 922/359-313; www.europcar.com
  Hertz tel: 922/759-319; www.hertz.es
  Cicar tel: 922/759-329; www.cicar.com

- It's useful to find out if you can rent a car in the airport and drop it off somewhere else.
- It's best to use one of the major car-rental companies as the **standard for servicing** some rental cars can be below average and there have even been reports of dangerous rental cars being allowed on the road.
- If you decide to rent a **moped** or **scooter** it is vital that you wear a crash helmet as these modes of transport are notorious for being involved in accidents.

Bus

- You can pick up public buses of **TITSA** (Transportes Interurbanos de Tenerife SA; www.titsa.com) to several destinations.
- **No 488** goes to Playa de las Americas via Los Cristianos. They run half hourly from 6:50am to 9:50pm (three services terminate at Los Cristianos

9:20am, 12:50pm and 3:20pm), with three night services. They take around an hour.

- **No 341** connects to Santa Cruz de Tenerife. Departures are approximately hourly from 6:50am and the journey takes about 90 minutes, straight up the *autopista*.
- **No 340** to Puerto de la Cruz leaves only four times a day and takes about one-and-a-half hours.

Taxi

- Taxi **fares** are reasonable to Los Cristianos or Playa de las Américas, but get expensive if you are trying to get to Santa Cruz de Tenerife or Puerto de la Cruz.

Tenerife Norte (Los Rodeos) Airport

The smaller Tenerife Norte (Los Rodeos) Airport in the north of the island (tel: 922/635-999) is mostly for inter-island flights and flights from mainland Spain. It is located 10km (6 miles) west of Santa Cruz de Tenerife and 26km (16 miles) east of Puerto de la Cruz. A complete overhaul has left it with a sparkling new terminal.

Transport from the Airport

Car Rental

- See above, Tenerife Sur (Reina Sofia) Airport, for general information on car hire.
- The same major car-rental companies (with the same contact numbers) are represented at Tenerife Norte (Los Rodeos) Airport.

Bus

- **TITSA bus No 107** runs a service between the airport and the centre of Santa Cruz de Tenerife every two hours Monday to Friday and four services a day at the weekend, terminating at the Estación de Guaguas, the main bus station. The trip takes about 30 minutes.
- **No 108** to Icod de los Vinos runs via La Orotava every two hours and takes an hour.
- **No 102** is a little slower and goes via La Laguna, 3km (2 miles) from Tenerife Norte Airport every 30 minutes or so. From the airport it continues west to Buenavista.
- **Buses** are generally an inexpensive way to travel around the island.

Taxi

- You can also get a taxi to **any destination** in the northeast of the island at a reasonable cost.
- Trips to Santa Cruz de Tenerife take 20 minutes and cost approximately €10–15.
- Trips to Puerto de la Cruz take 30 minutes are more expensive and typically cost €16–20.

Santa Cruz Estación Marítima (Ferry Terminal)

- The city's main **ferry port** is at the northeast end of town.
- Spains national ferry company, **Trasmediterránea** (tel: 902/454-645; www.trasmediterranea.es) runs ferries from Cádiz in Spain (once a week) plus a ferry service to Las Palmas de Gran Canaria (one per week), Arrecife (Lanzarote) (one per week), Puerto del Rosasio (Fuerteventura) (one per week), and Santa Cruz on La Palma (three times a week).

Fred Olsen Express (tel: 902/100-107; www.fredolsen.es) operates fast ferries to Gran Canaria (Ageate).
- **Other ferry companies** operate from quays a little closer to the town centre.
- It's a 10-minute walk to the centre of town from the main terminal, the **Muelle de Ribera**, or you can get a taxi for under €5.
- Boat **tickets** are available at most travel agents or direct from ferry companies' booths in the **Muelle de Ribera** building on the waterfront.

Los Cristianos Estación Marítima (Ferry Terminal)
- This is the **main point of arrival/departure** for boats from/to La Gomera, and the westernmost islands of La Palma and El Hierro.
- There are **one or two daily ferry** connections from El Hierro and La Palma.
- The ferry terminal is a **brisk walk** from the centre of Los Cristianos, where you will find banks, a tourist office and post office.
- A short bus ride takes you further around the coast to Playa de las Américas.

La Gomera
- **Binter Canarias** (tel: 902/391-391; www.bintercanarias.com) operates daily flights between La Gomera and both airports on Tenerife and two flights per day go to Gran Canaria.
- **Fred Olsen** (tel: 902/100-107; www.fredolsen.es) runs up to five daily fast ferries (approximately €16–20) to Los Cristianos (40 mins), and one car ferry (80 mins).
- **Garajonay Exprés** (tel: 902/343-450; www.garajonayexpres.com) has three fast ferries a day from Los Cristianos to San Sebastián de La Gomera with onward sailings to Playa Santiago and Valle Gran Rey, which cost about €16–20.

Orientation
- Tenerife is the largest of the Canary Islands, covering an area of around 2,000sq km (772 square miles).
- It's about 130km (81-miles) long at its widest part and about 90km (56 miles) north–south.
- About 300km (186 miles) separate the island from the coast of Morocco.
- Other islands in the **archipelago** include Lanzarote, Fuerteventura, Gran Canaria, La Gomera and La Palma.

Tourist Information Offices
- **Santa Cruz de Tenerife**: Cabildo Insular de Tenerife, Plaza de España s/n, 38003 Santa Cruz de Tenerife, tel: 922/239-592; Oct–Apr Mon–Fri 9–6, Sat 9–1; May–Sep Mon–Fri 9–5, Sat 9–12
- **La Laguna**: Plaza del Adelantado s/n, La Laguna, tel: 922/631-194; daily 9–5
- **La Orotava**: Calle Carrera Escultor Estévez 2, La Orotava, tel: 922/323-041; Mon–Fri 8:30–6
- **Puerto de la Cruz**: Plaza de Europa s/n, Puerto de la Cruz, tel: 922/386-000; Mon–Fri 9–8, Sat–Sun 9–5
- **Playa de las Américas**: Avenida Rafael Puig 1, Playa de las Américas, tel: 922/750-633; daily 9–5
- **San Sebastián de La Gomera**: Calle Real 4, San Sebastián, tel: 922/870-281; May–Oct Mon–Fri 8–8, Sat 9–1:30, 3:30–6, Sun 10–1; Nov–Apr Mon–Sat 9–1:30, 3:30–6, Sun 10–1

Getting Around

Although distances are not great, driving can be slow as roads are often winding and narrow. This is especially the case in mountainous areas in the northeast and northwest.

Buses

■ **TITSA** (Transportes Interurbanos de Tenerife SA) (tel: 922/531-300, www.titsa.com) runs a fairly efficient bus service all over the island. It also provides the local bus service in the bigger towns.

■ Buses are known as *guaguas* in Tenerife, but if you ask for the *autobús* people will know what you are talking about.

■ The main bus station on Tenerife is the **Estación de Guaguas** at Avenida de la Constitución at the corner with the avenida Tres de Mayo, 1.5km (1 mile) south of the city centre in Santa Cruz de Tenerife.

■ Bus stops in other conurbations, especially the tangle that is Los Cristianos, Playa de las Américas and Costa Adeje, are not always highly convenient for some hotels, so you may also need to get a taxi to get directly to the front door.

■ The **longest bus trips** (for instance Santa Cruz de Tenerife to Playa de las Américas) are still inexpensive (under €10).

■ If you plan to travel around the island extensively by bus, purchase a **Bono Bus** card for around €12 or €30. This gets you more for your money, as each trip you make is discounted by 50 per cent (30 per cent if 20km/12.5 miles or less). Insert the card into the bus ticket machine and the discounted fare is deducted when you tell the driver where you are going. If don't have enough money left on your card, you pay the driver the difference (at the discounted rate).

■ **Seven bus routes** (cover La Gomera, starting in San Sebastián and heading for Valle Gran Rey, Playa de Santiago and Hermigua. There are four or five daily runs except on Sunday when there are two or three.

Trams

■ Santa Cruz de Tenerife has a tram system (tel: 922/024-800; www.metrotenerife.com) with a single line that runs to La Laguna from 6am to midnight, with services every 30 minutes throughout the night on Fridays and Saturdays.

Driving

■ Drive on the **right**.

■ At the time of writing **speed limits** were under review so check current laws before you set off.

■ The blood **alcohol** limit is 0.05 per cent.

■ **Seat belts** must be worn by all passengers, and rear seatbelts must be worn if fitted.

■ **Fines** for traffic offences can be very high and foreigners can be obliged to pay on the spot.

■ The **standard of driving** is reasonable, although beware drivers who tend to be too impatient, particularly on bends on mountain roads. Never stop on narrow, winding roads to admire the view unless it is safe to pull off the road completely. *Miradores* (viewpoints) are placed every few kilometres specifically for this purpose.

■ **Petrol** is cheaper on Tenerife than in mainland Spain or other parts of Europe because of tax concessions for the Canary Islands. In Spanish **diesel** is *gasoleo* and **unleaded** is *sin plomo*.

- There are numerous **petrol garages** along main roads, with 24-hour opening in the larger resorts and towns. Many garages close on Sundays and public holidays. Don't drive into the mountains without a full tank as there are few, if any, petrol garages in remote areas.
- **Parking** in built-up areas such as Santa Cruz de Tenerife can be difficult, if not impossible.
- Most central areas have **meter parking**, but there are also **car parks**.
- In areas marked with blue lines – *zonas azul* (blue zones) – you must buy a parking ticket during the designated hours, usually between 9am and 2pm and 4pm and 8pm. If you forget, or exceed your time, you will receive a fine to be paid on the spot.
- Never leave anything visible in your car (rental cars attract particular attention) and preferably nothing of value even in the boot.

Taxis

- **Long trips**, such as between Puerto de la Cruz in the north and Playa de las Américas in the southwest, can be expensive, but there are set fares for many routes.
- Insist on the **meter** being properly set and/or establish a price with the driver before setting off.

Bicycles

- You can rent standard **bicycles** and **mountain bicycles** in some of the most visited areas.
- Bicycling is a rewarding way to get around the island, although you need to be fit to deal with some of the more **mountainous stretches**.
- Keep **water bottles** well filled as you can become quickly dehydrated in the heat.

Walking

- Walking is a great option in Tenerife and La Gomera and is growing in popularity, particularly in the **Parque Nacional del Teide** on Tenerife (➤ 118) and **Parque Nacional de Garajonay** on La Gomera (➤ 150).
- You can also go walking in plenty of other areas, such as the **Anaga mountains** in northeast Tenerife (➤ 73), around **Masca** in the northwest (➤ 100) and up the **Barranco del Infierno** in the southwest (➤ 158).
- Walking **maps** and **guidebooks** in various languages are available in bookshops in Santa Cruz de Tenerife and the tourist information offices around the island.

Boats

- Frequent **ferry** services run to La Gomera from Los Cristianos (➤ 32).
- Several **boat tours** allow you to get a seaside view of Tenerife (➤ 42).
- Apart from **dolphin-** and **whale-watching trips** operating mainly out of the southern resorts, you can also join **excursions** up the coast to see the Acantilado de los Gigantes (➤ 102).

Admission Charges
The cost of admission for museums and places of interest featured in the guide is indicated by the following price categories. Note that children aged 12 and above generally pay adult prices.

Inexpensive under €2　　　**Moderate** €2–5　　　**Expensive** over €5

Accommodation

The Canary Islands are Europe's most popular winter sun destination. On Tenerife more than 230 hotels, plus self-catering and timeshare complexes, are concentrated around a handful of intensively developed coastal strips. La Gomera has fewer places to stay, but even here the number of bed spaces is increasing to cater for its very different clientele.

Finding Somewhere to Stay

- Many hotels and apartments allocate all or most of their rooms to foreign **tour operators or travel agents**, and it can be difficult for independent travellers to find anywhere to stay at certain times of year. The February school holidays are particularly popular with visitors, who often coincide with an influx of Carnaval revellers (➤ 8).

- It's usually cheaper to arrange accommodation **in advance**, with air travel, some meals and perhaps car-rental or excursions included. But it's not impossible to find rooms on spec, depending on the time of year and how flexible you are about where you stay.

- The **equable climate** keeps Canarian hotels busy all year round, but the high season and highest prices generally occur between November and April.

- Lots of agencies in the main resorts specialise in property management for absentee owners. **Self-catering** or **timeshare** accommodation may be available to let at short notice. If possible, have a look at anything offered before committing yourself.

Types of Accommodation

Resort Hotels

- Most tourist hotels are **modern**, disguised to a greater or lesser degree by the island's lush subtropical vegetation. The overall picture is slightly more varied. The older resort of Puerto de la Cruz has several charming hotels in **traditional Canarian buildings** with timbered balconies.

- Package tourism is a vital mainstay of the economy, but **aesthetic considerations** are more of a priority in hotel building than they were in the 1960s and '70s. Gardens and pools are larger, architecture more diverse, and decor less stereotyped.

- The fast-expanding Costa Adeje area north of Playa de las Américas is targeting the upper end of the market and has hardly any budget accommodation. **Luxury complexes** like the extravagant Bahía del Duque (➤ 134) function as self-contained resorts.

- **La Gomera** has no huge resorts on the scale of Playa de las Américas. Apart from its *parador* and a single chic development on the south coast, the Jardín Tecina (➤ 154), accommodation is generally small and simple, suiting independent travellers who prefer more flexibility.

Self-Catering

- There's plenty of choice of **self-catering accommodation**, with around 260 complexes of apartments, bungalows or villas to rent on Tenerife, and around 130 on La Gomera.

- **Quality** is very variable.

- **Aparthotels** (apartment blocks with hotel facilities) combine the independence of a self-catering holiday with the advantage of not having to do the cooking all the time. Some have a minimum-stay requirement; most offer a regular maid service during your stay.

For more information on self-catering options contact the following:

- **Paradores de España** (*parador* centralised booking, Madrid): tel: 902/547-979; www.parador.es In the UK, **Keytel International** can arrange *parador* bookings; 402 Edgware Road, London W2 1ED; tel: 020 7616 0300; www.keytel.co.uk
- **Acantur** (Asociación Canaria de Turismo Rural); tel: 902/21582; www.ecoturismocanarias.com
- **Viajes Aecan**, Calle Villalba Hervás 2, Santa Cruz de Tenerife; tel: 922/248-114; www.cip.es/aecan
- **Camping Nauta**, Arona, Cañeda Blanca, Las Galletas; tel: 922/785-118; www.campingnauta.com
- **Secret Destinations** (UK-based operator; ask for the Secret Canaries brochure), tel: 0845 612 9000; www.secretdestinations.com
- **Casas Canarias** (London-based agency for self-catering properties); tel: 020 7558 8224; www.casascanarias.co.uk

Character Properties
- **Unusual types of accommodation**, such as a rural idyll on an old avocado farm, a taste of *grande luxe* in Santa Cruz and a B&B in a bishop's palace in Laguna, are little used by tour operators, so book them independently via the internet (► separate chapters).
- Both Tenerife and La Gomera have an attractive and very comfortable *parador* (part of Spain's state-run chain of high-class hotels). Though not cheap, they offer a memorable stay in wonderful settings. Tenerife's *parador* stands in the spectacular crater moonscapes of the Mount Teide National Park (► 133) and La Gomera's is in San Sebastián (► 153).

Rural Stays
- **Country hotels** and **self-catering cottage properties** (*casas rurales*) are increasing on both Tenerife and La Gomera.
- Some of these are charming old *fincas* (farmhouses) in beautiful inland settings. Standards are very variable, but the best are delightful.
- Some are used by special-interest tour operators as **walking bases**, but you'll probably need your own transport if you're travelling independently.

Budget Accommodation
- If funds are limited, there are modest rooms in a *pensión* or *hostal*. These are often older-style, family-owned establishments. Standards vary a lot. Though practically non-existent in the purpose-built surroundings of Playa de las Américas, you'll find them in the older quarters of Los Cristianos and Puerto de la Cruz, or in larger towns like Santa Cruz de Tenerife and San Sebastián on La Gomera.
- **Camping** possibilities are extremely limited.
- There are **no youth hostels** on either Tenerife or La Gomera.

Accommodation Prices
The following symbols indicate the price of a double room in high season, IGIC (Impuesto General Indirecto Canario) sales tax of 5 per cent is included. Rates vary seasonally.

€ under €70   €€ €70–120   €€€ over €120

Food and Drink

Assuming you aren't the sort of visitor cheered by signs announcing "No Spanish food here", you'll find plenty of places happy to serve you some genuine local specialities. Canarian cuisine is basically Spanish, with a difference. Many classic mainland dishes appear on the menu (gazpacho, paella, chorizo and tapas), but here hot chilli sauces mingle with a salty ocean tang or the tropical sweetness of bananas.

The Latin Connection

■ Since the time of Christopher Columbus, the Canaries have served as an Atlantic staging post between Spain and the Americas. It's hardly surprising many dishes have a Latin American flavour. Bananas, tomatoes, potatoes, peppers, sweetcorn, avocado, papaya – all South American crop-plants successfully transplanted to Tenerife – feature largely in local cooking.

■ The **hot chocolate potion** prized by Montezuma and the Aztecs appears transmuted into a sustaining breakfast dish used for dunking *churros* (sticks of sugary fried batter).

■ Look out, too, for a Venezuelan speciality called *arepas*, served in café-bars called *areperas*. These tasty little parcels of fried maize dough are stuffed with a variety of savoury fillings and offered with spicy dips. Two or three make an inexpensive bar snack.

A Taste of the Sea

■ Unsurprisingly, fish is a staple ingredient of all local diets, but many species are becoming scarce due to overfishing. Look out for typical varieties like the *vieja* (sun fish) or the *cherne* (bass).

■ Fish stews like *sancocho* or *zarzuela* are regular fixtures, but many good restaurants prefer to adapt their menus to whatever swims into the market that day.

■ *Papas arrugadas* (wrinkled jacket potatoes) are a ubiquitous Canary Islands side-order, perfect with fish. Traditionally cooked in seawater, they are now boiled in less bacterially challenged brine, which reduces their water content and intensifies the flavour, leaving a white crust of salt behind.

Regional Styles

■ **Soups** and **stews** are popular traditional dishes. Otherwise meat and fish are often best served *a la plancha* (grilled) or roasted. Rabbit, goat and suckling pig offer alternatives to steak, lamb and chicken.

■ Restaurants described as *típico* generally serve good home-cooking, and the chance to eat outside often adds to the pleasure.

■ Classic accompaniments to meat or fish dishes are the two kinds of spicy sauce known as *mojo*. *Mojo picón*, the red type, is a fiery recipe based on chilli and garlic; *mojo verde*, the green variety, is a less scorching concoction of coriander and parsley.

■ **Gofio** (toasted cereal meal) is a Canarian curiosity, allegedly the staple dish of the Guanches. Like other such survival rations eaten in times of plenty, its virtues can be overstated.

■ **Puddings** and **cakes** tend to be very sweet. *Bienmesabe* is a typical example, made with honey and almonds.

■ La Gomera is renowned for its tasty goat's cheese, smoked or flavoured with natural herbs.

Best...
...Castilian food: Los Cuatros Postes (➤ 61)
...coffee and cakes: Pastelaría El Aderno (➤ 111)
...classic cooking: El Drago (➤ 81)
...monastery setting: Méson El Monasterio (➤ 109)
...hotel restaurant: El Patio (➤ 135)
...terrace dining: Restaurante Pancho (➤ 110)
...traditional Canarian setting: El Rincón de la Piedra (➤ 62)
...wine: Casa del Vino La Baranda (➤ 80)
...valley view: Chez Arlette (➤ 110)

Drinks

- Canarian **wines** have improved enormously in the past decade or two, encouraged by more rigorous classification and regulation of the wine trade. Tenerife is the main producer, and most of its vines grow in the north of the island, especially around Tacoronte, Güímar and Icod de los Vinos. Interesting wines are produced on La Gomera too. For more information on wine, visit the **Casa del Vino La Baranda** (➤ 77).
- If you want to try a local spirit, look out for *ron* (rum), *cobana* (a banana-based liqueur) or *mistela* (a mead-like Gomeran invention made with honey or palm-syrup).
- The local **beer** is La Dorada. Ask for *a caña* (small glass) or *a jarra* (large) if you prefer draught beer.
- *Sangría* is on tap, though locals rarely touch it.
- **Coffee** is an art form in many different guises. Ask for *café solo* if you like it espresso-style, or *cortado* if you like a dash of milk. Locals like it made with condensed milk (*condensada*) or with a shot of alcohol – a *carajillo* or a *barraquito* are bracing pick-me-ups. *Café con hielo* is iced coffee.
- **Fresh fruit juices** are very popular; look for a *zumería* (juice bar) for exotic mixtures of papaya, avocado or mango, all locally grown.

When to Eat

- Meal times are **generally later** than in northern Europe. Lunch starts at 2pm and dinner at around 9pm, but resort hotels and restaurants often compromise to suit the preferences of their predominant clientele.
- Most restaurants offer an inexpensive *menú del día*, generally consisting of three rather ordinary courses with bread and a drink included. But it could be more enjoyable (though not necessarily cheaper) to have *tapas* in a bar.
- **Tax** and **service** are usually covered in the prices quoted, though a small tip is generally expected. Extra charges often apply if you sit outside at a terrace table.
- **Vegetarians** may find Canarian menus don't cater very well for them. A vegetarian diet seems to baffle most islanders.

Restaurant Prices
The € symbol indicates what you can expect to pay per person for a meal, including drinks, tax and tip.
€ under €20   €€ €20–40   €€€ over €40

Shopping

Tenerife's status as a mid-Atlantic duty-free bazaar has been eroded by EU legislation, but consumer goods continue to flood in to tempt holiday-makers with low prices.

Tax on Luxury Purchases

■ **Sales tax** on luxury items (IGIC) is still remarkably low compared with most European countries, including mainland Spain. Savings passed on to the customer, however, vary greatly from one outlet to the next. Alcohol and tobacco seem especially good value (locally produced cigars are popular), along with perfume and cosmetics, jewellery, leather, confectionery, cameras and binoculars, watches, electrical and electronic goods.

Duty Free?

■ Duty free does not mean tax free, but competition keeps resort prices low. Don't wait to do your shopping at the airport on your way home – the choice is limited and prices are higher than elsewhere on the island.

Where to Shop

■ *Mercados* (markets) come in all shapes and sizes, from daily cornucopias of fish, flowers and fruit to weekly flea markets (*rastros*) offloading miscellaneous junk. Street traders and stallholders hawk their wares along the seafront promenades wherever tourists are to be found.
■ For Canarian souvenirs, look for *centros de artesanía* (craft outlets), sometimes attached to workshops where the goods are actually made.
■ *Centros comerciales* (shopping centres) and Asian-owned bazaars are in all the big resorts, though large department stores and out-of-town hypermarkets are mostly confined to Santa Cruz de Tenerife.

Caveat Emptor (Buyer Beware)

■ Some stores **discourage haggling**, but prices are generally flexible – it's always worth asking for a discount.
■ Most tourist-orientated shops accept **credit cards**. It's a good idea to check slips carefully before you sign, and your subsequent statements.
■ Look out for signs saying *rebajas* (sales) or *liquidación* (closing-down sale) for especially low prices.
■ **Pirated** and **fake goods** are widespread in the Canaries. Few are well-crafted enough to deceive sophisticated shoppers, but it's best to avoid buying music recordings and videos or designer labels from market stalls or other dubious sources. If something looks too good to be a true, it probably is.
■ **Electronic equipment** for computers, mobile phones and the like is a risky purchase unless you have specialist technical knowledge. Some components may not be compatible with systems in the UK.
■ Not everything in the Canaries is a **bargain**. Do some price and product research before you leave home.
■ Don't sign up with a **timeshare tout**. If you want to invest in Canarian property, take sensible legal and financial advice.

Summer Craft Fairs

These fairs (*ferias de artesanía*), held in Tenerife's older inland communities, can be great fun if you're hunting for typical Canarian souvenirs. Dates vary from year to year; check with the tourist office.
■ **June**: Güímar, La Orotava, Los Realejos

- **July**: El Sauzal, La Laguna, Santiago del Teide
- **August**: Arona, Fasnia, Garachico, La Victoria de Acentejo, Buenavista del Norte, La Matanza
- **September**: Vilaflor, San Miguel de Abona, Guía de Isora, Tacoronte
- **October**: El Tanque

What to Buy

- **Embroidery** is a popular souvenir. The distinctive drawn-threadwork known as *calados* is often made into table- or bedlinen (placemats, pillowcases). It's an airy, openwork pattern that's on sale in markets and bazaars. Certified craft shops like **La Casa de los Balcones** are a reliable place to buy it. The main outlet in La Orotava has a working embroidery school and there are branches in several resorts.
- **Lace** is a speciality in the mountain village of Vilaflor. Genuine handmade products are expensive (beware of cheap machined goods imported from the Far East – they'll look a bit too regular). The best place to go to be sure of getting the genuine article is one of the authorised craft centres where you get a guarantee.
- **Leatherware** is an art form throughout Spain. You'll find bags, shoes, belts and wallets of variable quality on sale in all the resorts and markets.
- **Ceramics** based on traditional Guanche designs can be found both on Tenerife, especially at Arguayo near Los Gigantes, and at El Cercado on La Gomera. The classic style is made without a wheel and fired with a coating of red clay.
- Canarian **basketware** (*cestería*) takes a variety of forms; look out for souvenirs made from woven cane, straw, palm or banana leaves.
- Attractive bowls, dishes and spoons made from a variety of native trees make good **wooden** souvenirs, though much is made from imported olive-wood, which doesn't grow locally.
- *Chácaras* (castanets) make easy souvenirs to carry home, but you may see other Canarian musical instruments on sale, such as the stringed *timple*, in some craft outlets. Recordings of **local folk music** are often on sale at markets and craft centres.
- Avoid buying bladed objects or souvenirs made from endangered species (such as ivory, coral, fur and tortoiseshell). These may be impounded by customs when you go home.

Home-grown Produce

- **Edible souvenirs** include prettily packaged jars or bottles of green and red *mojo* or honey. On La Gomera, look out for *miel de palma* (palm syrup), and goat's cheeses preserved in oil.
- Biscuits, cakes and sweets, local wines or liqueurs made from **bananas** (*cobana*) or **honey** (*mistela* or *ronmiel*), and **cigars** made from local tobacco make other attractive souvenirs.
- Baby **dragon trees** (➤ 96) are on sale in many souvenir shops, though they are not frost-hardy. A genuinely worthwhile plant souvenir is a bunch of *strelitzia*, the flamboyant flame-and-navy 'bird of paradise' flowers. You can order these before your return journey, robustly packed and labelled to air-freight home.

Opening Times

- Standard shop opening times are Mon–Fri 9–1 and 4–8; Sat 9–2, but in tourist areas some outlets stay open much later, perhaps until 10pm, including Sundays. Most close during public holidays.
- **Markets** generally take place only in the **mornings**, and some start trading quite early.

Entertainment

What's On

Various multilingual newspapers are delivered free of charge to hotels. *La Gaceta de Canarias*, the weekly Canarian newspaper, has useful but random snippets on what's on. Other newspapers with information on what's going on include *Island Connections* and *Tenerife News*. Also worth looking out for is the Spanish-language monthly what's-on guide, *Lagenda*, available at news stands. Tourist offices can supply information on local fiestas, markets, sports facilities or cultural events.

Nightlife

If you're based in one of the big resorts, nightlife is impossible to avoid, especially in Playa de las Américas. Lots of organised evening entertainment goes on in the larger hotels.

- The top venue for spectacular **dinner-shows** (including flamenco) is the Pirámide de Arona (Mare Nostrum Resort, Los Cristianos, ➤ 137).
- The older quarters of Santa Cruz de Tenerife and Puerto de la Cruz are lively in the evenings, though here the emphasis is more on **strolling** and **dining**. Nightspots and elegant casinos are more discreetly located and patronised by locals as well as foreign visitors.
- At *Carnaval* time, however, the entire community erupts into festive mood that lasts for several days.
- Outside the resorts, nightlife is extremely limited or non-existent. Teide National Park's *parador* offers an awesome dose of starlit silence (➤ 133).

Outdoor Activities

- **Hang-gliding** (*parapente*), **rock-climbing** and **parascending** are readily on tap for the determinedly adventurous. Others may be content with a good **walk** (➤ 157), or a round of **golf** (➤ below).
- **Pot-holing** in one of the world's longest cave systems (the Cueva del Viento, near Icod de los Vinos) is a minority interest.

Spectator Sports

- Traditional Canarian trials of strength like *lucha canaria* (Canarian wrestling, ➤ 19) or *juego del palo* (stick fighting, ➤ 19) offer something different.
- Inevitably, there's also **football** (soccer).

Watersports

- A wide variety of watersports and activities – sailing, fishing, water-skiing, scuba diving, surfing, snorkelling, hiring of kayaks, pedaloes, jetskis and "banana boats" – compensate for the generally dark and stony beaches of the western Canaries.
- The best **diving** and **fishing** sites are near Los Gigantes, Las Galletas and south of Los Cristianos.

Golf

- Tenerife's oldest and smartest golf course is **RCG Tenerife** (Real Club de Golf) near La Laguna, dating from 1932 (➤ 82).
- Several newer courses are based in the south of the island, landscaped with cinder bunkers and palm trees, and with ocean views.
- The website www.webtenerife.com lists Tenerife's courses and facilities.
- Several **large hotels** offer golfing packages.

Walking

- **Spectacular terrain and wildlife** make Tenerife and La Gomera attractive to walkers.
- Both islands have **stunning mountain scenery** within their national parks, and hiking can easily be arranged along well-signed routes both for independent travellers or guided groups.
- Specialist operators organise **entire holidays** based on walking (sometimes featuring bird-watching and flower-spotting). Or you can join a guided hike to suit your own inclinations or fitness level when you arrive. A popular excursion combines a walk from Masca with a boat trip past the cliffs of Los Gigantes.
- If you prefer to do your own thing, maps with suggested walking routes are available from tourist offices and national park visitor centres. The website www.webtenerife.com has details and maps of 25 walks around the island that you can download.

Organised Tours

- If you don't want to rent a car, it's very easy to join an organised tour to see other parts of the island, and visit big-time tourist attractions like **Loro Parque** (➤ 104), **Castillo de San Miguel** (➤ 98) or **Teide National Park** (➤ 118).
- Other routes widely advertised take you to **Masca** and the **Teno Massif**, or to **Santa Cruz de Tenerife** for shopping.

Reservations

- Many holidaymakers join **organised activities** laid on by their hotels or tour companies.
- **Travel agencies and tourist offices** fill in the gaps. Tour operator notice boards display resort-based tourist entertainment, and you'll find dozens of ideas for excursions.
- If you're looking for **culture**, go to Santa Cruz de Tenerife or La Laguna; both have theatre and classical music programmes.

Boat Trips

- **Whale-** and **dolphin-watching** trips are big business off Tenerife's west coast. More than 20 species frequent these waters, particularly pilot whales and bottle-nosed dolphins. However, there is some evidence that the number of boats is causing disturbance and even injury, so choose a properly licensed operator.
- **Big-game fishing** excursions for shark, tuna or swordfish are also popular.
- **"Pirate cruises"**, beach picnics or barbecues generally include the cost of lunch and time for a swim.
- **The best boat trip** from Tenerife is a visit to La Gomera – a full day's outing from Los Cristianos. You can combine this with an organised coach tour, or see the island at your own pace (reserve ahead for car rental at San Sebastián docks – insurance doesn't allow you to take vehicles from one island to another).

Jeep Safaris

- Advertised in the main resorts, especially around Puerto Colón in Playa de las Américas, **off-road vehicles** take you through rugged terrain to remote parts of the island.

Santa Cruz de Tenerife

Getting Your Bearings

Humming with activity, Santa Cruz is the urban heart of Tenerife, far removed from the tourist clichés. A major port, it is the capital of the province (which includes the islands of La Gomera, La Palma and El Hierro) and home to 200,000 people, almost a third of Tenerife's population. It has two fine churches, a handful of curious museums, leafy squares, an aquatic centre and, just north of town, a fine beach.

There is another attraction. The Canary Islands are blessed with all sorts of tax breaks and the local version of sales tax – IGIC – is very low. As a result a good percentage of package tourists are guided through Santa Cruz for at least a morning's shopping.

One of the best parts about Santa Cruz is the chance to get lost in the bustle of a real Spanish city. There is enough to see and do to fill at least a day, and a little people-watching over a drink at a city centre *terraza* is the perfect way to while away an early afternoon. If you time your visit right you could be here for one of the most exciting festivals in the world – Carnaval. Since 2000, the city has undergone massive changes with a crop of contemporary buildings and communal spaces that have upped its cool factor. An enjoyable aquatic centre and a fine sandy beach just north of town add to the allure.

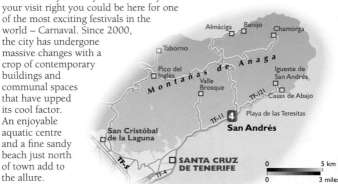

★ Don't Miss

Page 43: Yachts from all over arrive at Santa Cruz marina

Left: Christmas fireworks in Plaza de España, Santa Cruz

At Your Leisure

In a Day

If you're not quite sure where to begin your travels, this itinerary recommends a practical and enjoyable day out in Santa Cruz de Tenerife, taking in some of the best places to see using the Getting Your Bearings map on the previous page. For more information see the main entries.

10:00am

Begin in ❶ **Plaza de España** (➤ 48), where you can also pick up information at the tourist office in the Cabildo Insular building. Before heading into the city, wander along the waterfront for a while. Back in Plaza de España, the next logical step is to head up to ❶ **Plaza de la Candelaria** (➤ 49) and the shopping streets behind it.

11:30am

Head across to Plaza Isla de la Madera and visit the **Centro de Fotografía** before ducking down into the few streets that constitute what is left of old Santa Cruz. In ❷ **Plaza de la Iglesia** (➤ 50–52) visit the Iglesia de Nuestra Señora de la Concepción. Cross the Barranco de los Santos to the **Museo de la Naturaleza y El Hombre** (➤ 51), with its collection of Guanche mummies. Nearby is the city's big produce market, the ❼ **Mercado de Nuestra Señora de África** (➤ 58).

1:00pm

Have a typically Spanish lunch at Tasca Sáffron & Porron (➤ 62) on Calle Antonio Domínguez Alfonso.

2:30pm

After lunch, it's a quick walk across to **3 Plaza del Príncipe de Asturias** (➤ 53–54) for some local art appreciation at the Museo de Bellas Artes and a quick coffee at the Café del Príncipe. From here wander up Calle del Pilar to the **10 Parque García Sanabria** (➤ 59), where the *terrazas* are great for a drink, or further on to Rambla del General Franco (left).

3:30pm

If you feel the need to get out of the city, take a bus (Nos 245, 246, 247 or 910) or taxi up the coast to the inviting white sand beach of Las Teresitas (below) in **4 San Andrés** (➤ 55). During the week it's pretty quiet. If you have time and your own car, continue on to secluded **Playa de las Gaviotas** (➤ 56).

6:00pm

Return to Santa Cruz for an early evening view across the whole sweep of the port as you make your way back to the centre.

8:00pm

Try one of the restaurants or *tascas* in the streets south of the Hotel Contemporáneo. Keep an eye open for concerts at the **Teatro Guimerá** (➤ 64) and Auditorio de Tenerife (➤ 57) or, if you're looking for bars and clubs, try the long line-up of places along **Avenida Anaga**.

Plaza de España and Plaza de la Candelaria

These virtually interlocking squares are the most logical place to start exploring Santa Cruz de Tenerife. They are the administrative heart of Santa Cruz, right by the sea, and are worth wandering around to get a feel for the city, do a little shopping, have a snack or take a waterfront stroll.

Architectural Style

The **Plaza de España**, the central pivot of the seafront corniche has been given a makeover by the award winning architects Herzog and de Meuron who have created a stunning lake as the core feature. Overlooking this is a sombre war memorial raised to Spanish dictator General Franco flanked by monumental bronze statues and a triumphal ancient Greek-style open arcade. In the background rises the neo-classical headquarters of the government, the Cabildo Insular.

Originally laid out after Franco's rise to power, the new-look plaza, unveiled in July 2008, stands on the site where a defensive castle, the Castillo de San Cristóbal, had stood until its demolition in 1929. For about three weeks in February revellers flood Plaza de España and the surrounding streets as they celebrate the madness of **Carnaval** (▶ 8).

Carnaval overtakes Plaza de Espana in February

The square marks the halfway point of harbour-side Santa Cruz. To the southwest are the container docks, while to the northeast are a mix of ferries, cruise liners and merchant vessels compete for quay space. Further north still the container docks start again.

Away from the Harbour

Heading inland, **Plaza de la Candelaria** is more like a broad pedestrian boulevard connected to Plaza de España. The square, known as Plaza Real (Royal Square) and the Plaza de la Constitución (Constitution Square) until 1787, has lost much of the charm it once had. The northeast corner is dominated by the baroque Palacio de la Carta (now a bank), in whose interior lies a fine *patio* surrounded by timber balconies. On the same side of the square is the city casino. Watching over the centre of the square is a baroque statue of the Virgen de la Candelaria.

Grand ocean liners call in to Santa Cruz

The pedestrian streets that stretch inland from the square, especially **Calle Castillo**, are loaded with shops of all types, with a heavy bias towards electronic goods.

Right: Teatro Guimerá has been centre stage for 150 years

A short way off, on Plaza Isla de la Madera, is the **Teatro Guimerá** (➤ 64), built in the mid-19th century and named after Ángel Guimerá, a local dramatist. Inaugurated in 1851, the theatre is an example of the rich decoration of the era. In its heyday, it hosted peformances by companies en route from Europe to tour Latin America.

TAKING A BREAK

Try **Olympo** on Plaza de la Candelaria or **Mesón Los Monjes** (➤ 62) near Plaza de España.

➕ 183 E3

PLAZA DE ESPAÑA/PLAZA DE LA CANDELARIA: INSIDE INFO

In more depth The partnership of Jacques Herzog and Pierre de Meuron forms the heart of the **Herzog & de Mauron Architekten** architectural practice. Never afraid to innovate, they have a varied portfolio including the conversion of the old Bankside Power Station for the Tate Modern in London and the Beijing National Stadium, more commonly known as the "Bird's Nest", which was the centrepiece stadium for the 2008 Olympics.

2 Plaza de la Iglesia

Dominating the tiny oasis of old Santa Cruz is the city's most
striking church, Iglesia de Nuestra Señora de la Concepción,
while nearby a fine museum is another big attraction. Most
of Santa Cruz has succumbed to the 20th century, frequently
with little grace, but through the carefully maintained
traditional houses here you can be transported to the
colonial town of a bygone era.

Iglesia de Nuestra Señora de la Concepción

The **church** is recognisable from many points in the city by its
tall, elegant belfry, which is a mix of Portuguese baroque and
Moorish styles. There has been a church on this spot since the
end of the 15th century, although the original was destroyed
by fire during the 17th century.

The **facade** of the present church is another curiosity – an
atrium, topped by a fine timber balcony, precedes the main

**The Iglesia
de Nuestra
Señora de la
Concepción, at
the heart of old
Santa Cruz**

The rich *retablos* of Iglesia de Nuestra Senora

doorway. Built and altered over the 17th and 18th centuries, it is just as intriguing a mix on the inside, where five naves are divided by pillars and red stone arches.

To the right after you enter is the **Santa Cruz de la Conquista** (Holy Cross of the Conquest) that gave the city its name. The island's conqueror, Alonso Fernández de Lugo, planted the cross when he landed in 1494. The fine choir stalls were imported from London in 1862 and the alabaster pulpit is outstanding.

Much of the timber ceiling and other wooden elements of the church, such as the two *retablos*, were made from timber saved from a Spanish merchant vessel, *La Camorra*, which was sunk by English pirates in the 18th century.

Among the several paintings on display is the fine La Adoración de los Pastores (*Shepherds in Adoration*) by Juan de Miranda (1723–1805).

Museo de la Naturaleza y El Hombre

Across the usually dry Barranco de Santos (Santos Gorge) stands the austere former Hospital de la Caridad (Hospital of Charity), built in 1745 to attend to the poor and sick. Today it houses the Museo de la Naturaleza y El Hombre (Museum of Natural History and Man). Entrance to the museum takes you through the quiet courtyard of the former hospital.

The collections inside are wide ranging, although the emphasis is on Guanche civilisation and culture. The most engaging items are the **Guanche mummies** and skeletons and some of the more than 1,000 skulls found by archaeologists searching for clues to the island's pre-colonial past. Some of these show evidence of trepanning (holes drilled in the skull). There is no lack of possible explanations for why the Guanches carried out trepanning, but there seems to be no one certain reason. Among the other archaeological finds are tools, pottery fragments and jewellery.

Other displays cover **flora and fauna**, especially marine life, on the islands. More interesting is the ground-floor area devoted to the **volcanic history** of Tenerife and the other islands, which has a multimedia, multiscreen exhibition.

THE DEADLY SERIOUS BUSINESS OF DEATH

The Guanches were one of the few ancient peoples to mummify their dead (or at least those important enough to merit such treatment for the journey into the next life). It appears the Guanches had a horror of death and yet became expert in the art of embalming. This treatment was reserved mostly for dead chiefs and nobles, whose bodies were then laid out in distant burial caves. Although not as expert as the Egyptians, the Guanches must have carried out a reasonable enough job for some examples to survive to this day. Just how they learned these techniques and why they adopted them is a mystery. The embalmers themselves probably wondered what they had done to deserve such knowledge, since it appears they were considered by wider society to be almost as abhorrent as the corpses they handled.

TAKING A BREAK

Try out the **JC Murphy** Irish pub on Plaza de la Iglesia. The pub is housed in an impeccable traditional Canarian house and the terrace is the perfect spot for a drink. Or for a more substantial lunch there's **Cañas y Tapas** (➤ 61).

➕ 183 E2

Iglesia de Nuestra Señora de la Concepción
✉ Plaza de la Iglesia s/n 🕐 Daily 9–1, 5:30–8 💷 Free

Museo de la Naturaleza y el Hombre
✉ Calle Fuente Morales s/n ☎ 922/535-816 🕐 Tue–Sun 9–7
💷 Moderate

PLAZA DE LA IGLESIA: INSIDE INFO

Top tip In the anteroom of the sacristy in the Iglesia de Nuestra Señora de la Concepción is a fine **chapel**. It was paid for by Don Matías Carta, a prominent local citizen, whose portrait can be found in the sacristy. It was painted after his death, which explains the pallor and pose.

3 Plaza del Príncipe de Asturias

The cradle of Canary Island art is the Museo de Bellas Artes (Fine Arts Museum), which faces the leafy square of Plaza del Príncipe de Asturias in the city centre. Next door stands the Iglesia de San Francisco, an impressive baroque church.

Museo de Bellas Artes

Down a flight of stairs you arrive in Calle José Murphy, which forms the southern boundary of the square. Here stands the city library, which also houses the Museo de Bellas Artes.

The best way to visit the museum is to head directly to the top floor. In the first room are several **sculptures**, including one of the South-American revolutionary Simón Bolívar. To the right is a display of art from the 16th to the 18th century. A great deal of it is by unknown artists, but a few paintings stand out, like a portrait of St Andrew (San Andrés) presumed to be by José Ribera (1591–1652).

Back in the first room, a series of halls straight ahead is dedicated to **Canary Islands artists** of the 19th century. The first two rooms are dedicated to landscapes and portraits by Nicolás Alfaro (1826–1905) and his student, Valentín

Detail from the facade of the Círculo de Amistad XII de Enero on Plaza del Príncipe de Asturias

Sanz Carta (1849–98). Both painted scenes in the islands and in continental Europe.

Another major painter of the era was Manuel González Méndez (1843–1909), whose portraits, including a striking image of a Güímar boatman in red headgear and earrings, fill one of the rooms.

On the first floor is a statue of a *lechera canaria,* a milkmaid with canisters on her head. The rest of the floor is a mix of **19th-century Canarian painters** and a hall devoted to modern art from the islands. Among some of the more interesting artists whose work portrayed typical Tenerife themes is Alfredo Torres Edwards (1889–1943), whose striking scene of island women in traditional dress stands out.

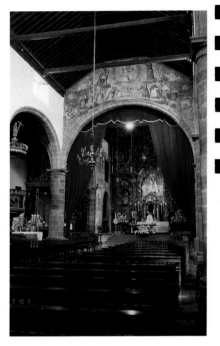

Iglesia de San Francisco

Next door to the museum is the ochre rear wall of the Iglesia de San Francisco. The **baroque façade** is typical of the island, a combination of dark stone and whitewash. Founded in 1680, the church is divided into three aisles separated by arches and a timber *artesonado* ceiling that resembles the upturned hull of a boat.

The Iglesia de San Francisco's roof is a wooden work of art

TAKING A BREAK

After filling up on art in the Museo de Bellas Artes, sip a coffee in the **Café del Príncipe**, right on the plaza.

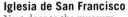

➕ 183 D3

Museo de Bellas Artes
➕ 183 E3 ✉ Calle José Murphy 12, Plaza del Príncipe ☎ 922/244-358
🕐 Tue–Fri 10–8pm, Sat–Sun 10–3 💲 Free

Iglesia de San Francisco
➕ 183 E3 ✉ Calle Villalba Hervás s/n 🕐 Mon–Fri 9–1, 5:30–8 💲 Free

PLAZA DEL PRÍNCIPE: INSIDE INFO

Top tip Also facing Plaza del Príncipe de Asturias is the **Círculo de Amistad XII Enero**, a marvellous Second-Empire caprice built in 1904 as home to a private social club. It remains so today, which means you can only admire its extraordinary facade from the outside.

4 San Andrés

Santa Cruz's escape route is a short drive to the north – the cheerful town of San Andrés and neighbouring white beach of Playa de las Teresitas. Head up into the hills north of the beach to discover an even more secluded beach, Playa de las Gaviotas. A little further still leads you to a typical Canarian town, Igueste, from where you could set out on a couple of hill country walks.

San Andrés huddles at the end of Playa de las Teresitas

Despite its proximity to Santa Cruz, which is barely 8km (5 miles) southwest, **San Andrés** has retained its fishing-village atmosphere. With one of the island's best beaches, **Playa de las Teresitas**, just 1km (0.5 miles) further on, the *pueblo* (town) is the perfect place to fall back on after you

tire of sand. Locals from Santa Cruz fill the restaurants with lively conversation. It makes a pleasant change to feel that the "tourists" catered for are predominantly local.

The town is guarded by a semi-ruined round tower fort, known as the *castillo* (castle). Wander into the central shady square, surrounded by bars and a small 18th-century chapel of red stone and whitewash. Behind, rows of houses struggle up the hillside, looking from afar like an unsteady pyramid.

The Beaches

Playa de las Teresitas is an artificial marvel. Proving that the 1970s were not all bad taste, the island's government bought 100,000 cubic metres (130,950 cubic yards) of Saharan sand to create a nice beach for the locals, protected by a breakwater.

Palm trees stud the inland strip of this broad strand, providing welcome shade. More palms virtually hide the parking strip and handful of seafood restaurants just behind the beach.

Igueste

Four kilometres (2.5 miles) northeast of **Playa de las Gaviotas**, the TF11 road ends in the silent farming village of Igueste. Along with other villages scattered across the Anaga mountain range (➤ 73–75), Igueste takes you light years from the pounding tourist resorts of the south. This is the real Tenerife, and before the arrival of tourists in the 1960s, was Tenerife. The village, looking like someone has randomly cast a box of white dice about the countryside, ranges up on either side of a *barranco* (gorge), in whose often dry bed the people grow everything from bananas to avocados and potatoes.

Palms provide a tropical touch at Playa de las Teresitas

TAKING A BREAK

There is no shortage of restaurants just back from **Playa de las Teresitas**. Or test out **Marisquería Ramon** (➤ 62) in San Andrés itself.

➕ 181 E4

At Your Leisure

5 Castillo de San Juan and Auditorio

Virtually next door to Manrique's fanciful Parque Marítimo (below) is the ageing and more prosaic Castillo de San Juan, one of the city's old defensive forts. Built in 1679 of the local dark basalt and now closed to the public, this circular reminder of the early days of Santa Cruz's history is known as the **Castillo Negro** (Black Castle). In the old days the fort was outside the city walls and, under the watchful eye of its garrison, slave traders sold black Africans, most of whom were later transported to the Caribbean to be used as forced labour on the sugar plantations.

Just east of the fort, a new monument to modern culture has emerged. The **Auditorio de Tenerife**, designed by Santiago Calatrava as the city's star concert hall, has the appearance of a gigantic white spinnaker on its back. Calatrava (1951–) is one of Spain's most prominent architects. With a background in structural engineering he creates buildings that stretch the design envelope – working in sensual curves such as at the Cuitat de les Arts y les Ciències in Valencia or the Turning Torso building in Malmo, Sweden. However, the Auditorio is one of his most striking buildings.

Across the busy highway another remnant from the past is the tiny red-and-white **Ermita de la Virgen de la Regla**, built in 1643. It could not look more out of place, surrounded by building sites, as this entire quarter of the city is transformed into a sea of mid-level and high-rise residential housing.

➕ 183 D1 (off map) ✉ Avenida de la Constitución s/n

6 Parque Marítimo

Designed by the Lanzarote artist César Manrique (1919–92), who is something of a legend in the Canary Islands, the Parque Marítimo is like a painting or carefully crafted garden, although people relax here as if it were just their local swimming pool. The small shallow lakes are opal blue and dotted with palms and carefully placed rock groups. There are a couple of cafeterias and restaurants and the whole thing is startlingly reminiscent of the Lago Martiánez in Puerto de la Cruz (➤ 93). During the week in winter the place is often close to empty. Just to the south stretches the **Palmetum**, a palm park (some say it is the largest in the world) with 5,000 trees and 300 species.

➕ 183 D1 (off map) ✉ Avenida de la Constitución s/n ☎ 922/202-995 🕐 Summer daily 10–7; winter daily 10–6 💰 Moderate

César Manrique created a crystal-clear water paradise right by the Atlantic Ocean in Santa Cruz

7 Mercado de Nuestra Señora de Africa

The Market of Our Lady of Africa is a typical Spanish-produce market, spread out across interconnecting *patios*. You can find everything from fruit and nuts to ham and cheese, and much else besides. An

Locals flock to the Mercado de Nuestra Señora de Africa, the main fresh produce market in Santa Cruz

underground level also contains a separate *pescaderia* (fish market). To mix in with the melée of locals and absorb the sights, sounds and smells is to get a taste of the real Spain. Alongside the market, a diverse flea market is held every Sunday – a few stalls are open during the week too.

➕ 183 D2 ✉ Plaza de Santa Cruz de la Sierra s/n 🕐 Daily 6–3

8 Tenerife Espacio de las Artes (TEA)

Opened in late 2008, this spectacular public space links several of the city's leading arts organisations to create a new focus in the city. Designed by Hertzog and de Mauron, the "arts space" incorporates 2ha (5 acres) and houses the Oscar Dominguez Institute of Contemporary Art and Culture, the Tenerife Center for Photography and Alejandro Cioranescu Insular Library.

➕ 183 D2 ✉ Avenida de San Sebastian ☎ 922/849-057, www.teatenerife.es 🕐 Tue–Sun 10–8 💷 Moderate

Ceramic benches and fountain bring a splash of colour to Plaza 25 de Julio

9 Plaza 25 de Julio

Better known as Plaza de los Patos (Ducks' Square), this soothing refuge is named after the date of Nelson's defeat in 1797. The bright central fountain, in *mudéjar* style (a Moorish-influenced style of architecture and decoration), is crowned by a duck and surrounded by ceramic frogs. The most attractive elements are the public benches, covered in ceramics advertising the companies that paid for them at the beginning of the 20th century.

🞧 182 C4 ✉ Halfway along Avenida de 25 de Julio

10 Parque García Sanabria

This city park is packed with a variety of tropical and sub-tropical trees and plants, a series of soothing fountains, a handful of modern sculptures left over from an urban art competition and benches for the weary. It represents a rare escape from the noise and chaos of the surrounding city. The central fountain serves also as a monument to Mayor García Sanabria, who ordered the creation of the park in 1922. The southern end livens up in the evening as people gather for a drink in the *terrazas* and children play on the swings.

🞧 182 C4 ✉ Between La Rambla del General Franco and Calle Méndez Núñez

11 Museo Militar

Housed in the former fortress of the Almeida, the Museo Militar takes centre stage in what remains a military post. You will be escorted from the gate by a soldier and, once inside, ushered to the top floor where there's a display telling the story of Nelson's abortive assault on Santa Cruz in 1797 (➤ 17). It becomes clear as you wander around the museum that this was the Canary Islands' proudest military moment.

Working your way around the semicircle, first up is a display of Spanish flags and ensigns, followed by an array of weapons and medals and on to an extensive section that is dedicated to the heroic defence of the city against Nelson.

Peace and quiet in Parque García Sanabria

Dioramas, paintings and maps all play their part in explaining the battle in detail, which is completed by such items as the instrument of British surrender and a copy of the maps drawn by Nelson himself to summarise the battle. The centrepiece is the *Tigre*, the cannon they say blew off Nelson's right arm, accompanied by a captured British flag and rifles.

The last part of the top floor is taken up with souvenirs of the Canary Islands' heroes of the Civil War and a small display on the Philippines and Cuba, which Spain lost to the US in the disastrous year of 1898 when the US sent Spain's navy to the bottom of the sea.

The ground floor is dedicated to weapons and other souvenirs from various colonial wars. The courtyard is lined with artillery pieces.

🞧 183 E5 ✉ Calle San Isidro 2 ☎ 922/843-500 🕐 Tue–Sat 10–2 🎟 Free

Where to... Stay

Prices

The following price ranges are for a double room in high season, IGIC sales tax included. Rates vary seasonally.

€ under €70   €€ €70–120   €€€ over €120

If you're intending to stay in Santa Cruz at Carnaval time (mid-February), book well ahead and expect to pay over the odds for a room.

Atlántico €

It's hard to find anything much more central than this friendly, inexpensive place just a stone's throw from Plaza de España. If it's a little old-fashioned, the Atlántico makes a perfectly acceptable base for a short stay. There's no restaurant, but the lively upstairs terrace café-bar overlooking the pedestrianised shopping street outside is one of its main assets – a popular meeting place for simple snacks and drinks. The modest rate charged for the 60 rooms includes breakfast.

➕ 183 E3 ⊠ Calle Castillo 12
☎ 922/246-375

Contemporáneo €€

Easy to find on the main thoroughfare through the town centre, this pleasingly designed business hotel makes a comfortable and practical choice. As the name suggests, it's a modern building with a sophisticated air. There's air-conditioning and TV in all 126 rooms. Passing traffic is noisy, but the interior is well insulated, and next to the hotel lies the cool, green Parque García Sanabria, an oasis of birdsong and flame-trees (▶ 59). The bar-café and restaurant provide a stylish stop. Rooms are sleek and well equipped.

➕ 182 C5 ⊠ Rambla General Franco 116
☎ 922/271-571;
www.hotelcontemporaneo.com

NH Tenerife €€

This ultra contemporary hotel with its clean design of glass and metal is by far the coolest place in town. Though not expansive, the rooms feel spacious with a black-and-grey colour scheme and come complete with flat-screen TV and full-length window. The garden lounge bar is an excellent place to while away the evening, though the delights of the city are just on the doorstep. There's

also an excellent bistro, Nhube, on site (▶ 62), a bar, gym, Jacuzzi and sun deck. The atmosphere is definitely more of adult/business hotel than a family resort.

➕ 183 E3 ⊠ Candelaria Esquina Doctor Allart ☎ 922/534-422; www.nh-hotels.com

Taburiente €€

This central hotel isn't particularly old, but an aura of old-world grandeur clings to its marble hall and classic furnishings. Impressive facilities include air-conditioning, TV, a gym, sauna, tennis and squash courts, garage parking – even a heated rooftop swimming pool. Despite this, its tariff remains surprisingly moderate. Many of the 116 rooms have attractive views over the neighbouring Parque García Sanabria (▶ 59). All rooms have safes and fridges. The restaurant offers a broad international menu.

➕ 183 D5 ⊠ Avenida Doctor José Naveiras 24A ☎ 922/276-000;
www.hoteltaburiente.com

Where to...
Eat and Drink

Prices

The following price ranges indicate what you can expect to pay per person for a meal, including drinks, tax and tip.

€ under €18   €€ €18–36   €€€ over €36

SANTA CRUZ DE TENERIFE

Bulan €–€€

Bulan is inside a typical old Santa Cruz house that has been injected with a vaguely Oriental chillout ambience. Diners congregate in one of the labyrinth of cosy dining areas on the ground floor for Eastern-influenced cuisine. The pinchos Katmandu are chicken chunks served in a peanut sauce with a splash of honey. You can just sit around the bar or head upstairs to the airy roof terrace...and two more bars.

⊞ 183 D5 ⊠ Calle Antonio Dominguez Alfonso 35 ☎ 922/274-116; www.bulantenerife.com ⊚ Daily 12:30–4, 8pm–1am

Cañas y Tapas €€

Along the seafront by the harbour, this Canarian outpost of a mainland tapas-bar chain packs in the crowds as the shadows lengthen. Some earthy Spanish offerings such as pulpo (octopus) and chorizo (spicy sausage) are on its long menu. The surroundings are a classic blend of dark wood and tiles. Groups willing to share get the best value, as individual portions can soon clock up an alarming bill. There are some tables set up outside.

⊞ 183 F5 ⊠ Avenida de Anaga 15 ☎ 922/246-972 ⊚ Sun–Wed noon–2am, Thu–Sat noon–3am

Clavijo Treinta y Ocho €€€

The verdant courtyard garden off this traditional restaurant makes a wonderful location for an al fresco lunch or dinner. The menu concentrates on Spanish dishes, including excellent meats, matched by a fine list of mainland Spanish and local Canarian wines. The ambience here is conducive to a long slow meal and service is relaxed.

⊞ 182 C4 ⊠ Calle Vierra y Clavijo 38 ☎ 922/271-065 ⊚ Mon–Sat 1–4, 8–midnight

El Coto de Antonio €€

Established as a smart and reliable favourite with discerning locals and business clients, this restaurant offers simple but elegantly contemporary decor. The cuisine is solid and authentic – a mix of Canarian and Basque styles. Look out for vieja (local sunfish) and sancocho (seafood stew) or codillo de cerdo (pig's trotters) if you're feeling a bit more adventurous. One of the house specialities is pejines (sun-cured fish marinated in alcohol and then flambé).

⊞ 182 A4 ⊠ Calle General Goded 13 ☎ 922/272-105 ⊚ Mon–Sat 1–4, 8–midnight; closed in late Aug or early Sep for two weeks

Los Cuatros Postes €€–€€€

One of the finest Castilian restaurants in town has a loyal local fan base and is always busy at lunch-times. This is one place to come and enjoy the atmosphere of a genuine Spanish midday dining experience – but remember to make a reservation. The menu includes excellent roasted meats, locally caught fish and luxury ingredients like foie gras.

🔲 183 E3 ⌧ Calle Emilio Calzadilla 5 🕾 922/287-394 ⌚ Mon–Sat noon–4, 8–midnight. Closed Sun

El Líbano €€

This is an excellent Lebanese spot hidden away in a side street, but much sought after at lunchtime by local *aficionados*. A comprehensive menu features well-known fare like kebabs and vine leaves, but strays into less familiar territory with a fine selection of vegetarian dishes.

🔲 183 E5 ⌧ Calle Santiago Cuadrado 36 🕾 922/285-914 ⌚ Daily noon–4, 8–midnight

Mesón Los Monjes €€

This is a well-regarded restaurant handily located just north of Plaza de España. At lunchtime its clientele consists mostly of business people, while families make their way here for dinner. The split-level dining areas are decorated in rustic Castilian style with plain walls and lots of woodwork. House specialities include Basque and

mainland Spanish recipes like *merluza con mojo* (hake with spicy sauce). Look out for the celebrated Ribero del Duero wines.

🔲 183 E4 ⌧ Calle La Marina 7 🕾 922/ 246-576 ⌚ Mon–Sat 1:30–3:30, 8–midnight

Mesón el Portón €€

Get down to this typical Canarian eatery for hearty fare. Locals opt either for the restaurant section, beneath exposed beams, at tables set with linen, or the more rough-and-tumble *tasca* next door, a bar where you can dine among the cheerful drinking fraternity. In a location away from the tourist waterfront, it is a touch of the real Tenerife.

🔲 183 D5 ⌧ Calle Doctor Guigou 20 🕾 922/280-764 ⌚ Mon–Sat 11–11

Nhube €€–€€€

The cool marble floors, full-length glass walls and designer furniture in this contemporary eatery match the modern fusion theme of chef Ferrán Adrià's menu. At lunch time is it

popular with the power-lunching crowd and evenings see young fashionable locals. It's a place to see and be seen.

🔲 183 E3 ⌧ Candelaria Esquina Doctor Allart 🕾 922/534-422; www.nh-hotels.com ⌚ Mon–Sat 7–11 (for buffet breakfast), 11–11 for à la carte; Sun 8–noon (for buffet breakfast), noon–11 for à la carte

El Rincón de la Piedra €€–€€€

Renowned for its charming setting – a lovely old Canarian house with fine timbers and carved woodwork – this rambling restaurant has a friendly atmosphere. It offers well-prepared Canarian specialities such as local fish, crisp, fresh salads and huge *solomillo* (steaks).

🔲 182 B3 ⌧ Calle Benavides 32 🕾 922/ 249-778 ⌚ Mon 7:30pm–11:30pm, Tue–Sat noon–4:30, 7:30–11:30

Tasca Sáfron & Porron €–€€

This boisterous eatery seems taller than it is wide. Housed in a classic building in what remains of old Santa Cruz, it oozes a

spanking Spanish vibe, with bullfight posters on the walls and a flamenco soundtrack. The menu is a seafood snack parade from big red carabinero prawns to chunky *navajas* (razor clams).

🔲 183 D2 ⌧ Calle Antonio Domínguez Alfonso 36 🕾 922/151-867 ⌚ Tue–Thu, Sun 1–4:30, 8–midnight; Fri–Sat 1–4:30, 8–1:30

Marisquería Ramón €€

Ramón specialises in locally caught seafood and is one of the most reputable restaurants behind Playa Las Teresitas. What better way to interrupt a lazy day on one of Tenerife's most glorious beaches than by sampling some of the chef's delicious creations? Or fortifying yourself for an excursion into the Anaga Mountains? Reflecting its location, the interior here is simple, light and bright.

🔲 181 E4 ⌧ Calle Dique 23 🕾 922/549-308 ⌚ Daily noon–11

Where to... Shop

Santa Cruz owes its trading success to nearly 150 years of "free port" status. Cruise passengers disembark for a spree in the shops close to the harbour, and excursion trips from the main resorts are sold as shopping expeditions. Most shops are on or around Plaza de la Candelaria and the pedestrianised Calle Castillo. Many close on Sunday, public holidays and in the afternoon (1–5pm), so arrive early.

BOUTIQUES AND BAZAARS

Shops selling perfume, alcohol and tobacco lure customers with "duty-free" or "tax-free" price tags in the streets near the port. Locally made *puros* (cigars) are a popular buy.

Many bazaars specialise in rugs, jewellery, porcelain, silks, watches, cameras, mobile phones and optical and electronic gadgets. You can always try for a discount on marked prices, though some stores decline to haggle. Remember electrical products or computer components may not be compatible with what you have at home.

Clothing outlets compete with the big department stores, selling everything from inexpensive jeans to designer sportswear. The classier fashion boutiques lie a little further from the waterfront, on and around Calle Castillo.

DEPARTMENT STORES

Santa Cruz has branches of mainland Spain's big chain department stores like El Corte Inglés, with a big branch one block west of the bus station, Cortefiel, and a local store called Maya. All sell food and wine, men's and women's clothing, luggage, home wares, electronics and so forth.

Huge out-of-town hypermarkets like Continente cater for local needs at bargain-basement prices (Autopista del Sur, Santa María del Mar exit, 6km/3.5 miles south). Other large shopping centres with Las Chumberas and Alcampo (off the motorway to La Laguna).

CRAFTS AND LOCAL PRODUCE

The large selections and fair prices of several reputable *artesanía* stores within five minutes' walk of each other make Santa Cruz a good place for gifts and souvenirs – though they lack the local interest of specialist craft-producing centres such as La Orotava (▶ 88).

The following outlets are worth a visit for **typical crafts** such as embroidery, lace, basketwork, woodcarvings, dolls in Canarian costumes and food products like honey and spicy *mojo sauce*: Arte Tenerife, Plaza de España; Artesanía Celsa, Calle Castillo 8; Casa de los Balcones, Plaza de la Candelaria.

MARKETS

A visit to Santa Cruz's daily fresh-produce market is one of the most entertaining aspects of shopping in the capital. The vibrant stalls of the **Mercado de Nuestra Señora de Africa** (Daily 6–3) are a fascinating sight (▶ 58). There are 300 stalls brimming with a pungent cornucopia of fruit, vegetables, meat and fish, flowers, herbs and spices, cheese, live rabbits and poultry. On Sunday mornings, **Rastro**, a lively flea market, is held in the streets near by, offering a vast range of interesting housewares, clothing and junk. (Beware of pickpockets who thrive on the crowds here.)

Where to...
Be Entertained

Local newspapers like *Tenerife News* or *La Gaceta* tell you what's on when or check out the local tourist information office.

OVERVIEW

The central monument is the starting point for a small **tourist train** that trundles round the historic city centre (every hour from 10am). The **tourist office** is in the Cabildo Insular on Plaza de España (tel: 922/239-592, Oct–Apr Mon–Fri 9–6, Sat 9–1; May–Sep Mon–Fri 9–5, Sat 9–noon).

THEATRE AND CONCERTS

Santa Cruz's two main venues for performing arts are the hyper-modern **Auditorio de Tenerife**

(▶ 57, Avenida de la Constitución, Box office: tel: 902/317-327, general: tel: 922/568-600; www. auditoriodetenerife.com) and the classic **Teatro Guimera** (Calle Imeldo Seris, tel: 902/364-603; www.teatroguimera.es).

FESTIVALS AND EVENTS

Santa Cruz's **Carnaval** dwarfs all other events in the Canaries. This fantastic jamboree lasts for several weeks. Each year a different theme is chosen for the parade floats, but the bizarre Ash Wednesday procession known as the "Funeral of the Sardine" is a regular fixture. A huge, brightly decorated and highly combustible fish effigy is carried through the streets to the mock wails of costumed mourners,

then set alight near the harbour with fireworks and dancing.

New Year starts with a party in the main square; as the clocks chime midnight, each reveller tries to swallow 12 grapes. The **Cabalgata de los Reyes Magos** (Epiphany, 5–6 Jan) and **Semana Santa** (Holy Week) are celebrated with colourful Spanish processions.

The **international music festival** (Jan–Mar) is a well-known draw throughout the islands. On 25 August, Santa Cruz combines the **Feast of St James** (Spain's patron saint, Santiago Apóstolo) with a good-humoured thanksgiving for the defeat of Nelson who attacked the city in July 1797 (▶ 14).

ON THE WATERFRONT

Beyond San Andrés is one of the island's most beautiful beaches, **Playa de las Teresitas** (▶ 56), a sheltered belt of Saharan sand. To the south of Plaza de España, near the Castillo de San Juan is a lido complex

of swimming pools, the **Parque Marítimo** (▶ 57). For information on watersports, contact the **Club Nautico** (Avenida de Anaga, tel: 922/273-700; www.rcnt.es).

NIGHTLIFE

Santa Cruz's central plazas buzz with cafés and bars all day and night. Most nightspots are on **Avenida Anaga**, the waterfront boulevard leading north of the centre) and **Rambla General Franco**. Among the better options are Musa (Avenida Anaga) for cocktails, and Klan-D-Stino (Avenida Anaga 31) for a young dance scene.

Hotel Mencey (Avenida Doctor José Naveiras 38) has a **casino** (take your passport and dress smartly); slot machines open at 4pm, gaming tables at 8pm.

Santa Cruz's **bullring** (Plaza de Toros) is never used for bullfighting, but is being refurbished as a multi-use exhibition space.

La Laguna and the Northeast

Getting Your Bearings

The northeast tip of Tenerife, explored by only a small percentage of the millions of visitors to the island each year, packs a lot into a small area, from mountain walks in the Anaga range to surfing off the north coast, and from the pretty old city of La Laguna to the centre of the archipelago's wine industry. The climate here can be cool and unpredictable.

Barely 10km (6 miles) inland from Santa Cruz is the city that, until well into the 18th century, was capital of the entire archipelago – La Laguna. An important university centre, La Laguna has preserved its intriguing town centre but also has a thriving student nightlife scene.

To the north and east stretch the rugged Montañas de Anaga (Anaga Mountains), with fine walks and interesting tours (▶ 73). Among the sights in the mountain range are the isolated coastal village of Taganana and the cave dwellings of Chinamada. Along the north coast are several small beaches and settlements – surfers flock to this part of the island.

On the road west of La Laguna you are in wine country. You can learn more in the area's wine museum near El Sauzal (▶ 77) and explore a couple of the little towns along the old Puerto de la Cruz road. South of La Laguna a lovely road winds inland through the Bosque de la Esperanza towards Mount Teide (▶ 118–122).

Punta del Guincho

Punta del Hidalgo 8

Bajamar 8

Tejina

Casa de Carta 7

Valle de Guerra

El Socorro · Las Mercedes · Tegueste

Guamasa · **San Cristóbal de la Laguna**

Los Rodeos ✈

El Sauzal 6 6 · **Tacoronte** 5 · TF-5

Stunt Galeria de Arte 1 3

TF-24 · Barranco de las Lajas

Casa del Vino la Baranda · Agua García

La Esperanza · TF-2

La Matanza de Acentejo · Mirador Pico de las Flores · Santa María del Mar

La Victoria de Acentejo · 4 · **Bosque de la Esperanza**

Barranco Hondo · TF-1

Mirador de Ortuno

Page 65: A flight of steps outside the town hall in El Sauzal

Left: Fishing boats at Punta del Hidalgo

**Above: Walkers in the
Montañas de Anaga
near Chinamada**

**Right: Dense forests of
Canary pine line the way
through the Bosque de
la Esperanza**

In Two Days

If you're not quite sure where to begin your travels, this itinerary recommends two practical and enjoyable days out in La Laguna and the Northeast, taking in some of the best places to see using the Getting Your Bearings map on the previous page. For more information see the main entries.

Day One

9:00am

Start in Plaza del Adelantado in **❶ La Laguna**, from where you can indulge in a relaxed morning walking tour of the city's old centre (➤ 70). The most straightforward walk takes you north along Calle Obispo Rey Redondo past the cathedral and up to the **Iglesia de la Concepción**. From there move east a block and go back along **Calle San Agustín**, along which you can admire some of the city's finest colonial mansions. Set aside an hour for the **Museo de Historia y Antropología de Tenerife** in the Casa Lercaro.

12:30pm

If you can accustom yourself to Spanish eating times and hang on a little before lunch, drive west to **❺ Tacoronte** (➤ 77), Tenerife's wine capital and worth a little wander. Make for the centre of town and the **Iglesia de Santa Catalina** (below).

2:00pm

After a short drive further west you reach the turn-off for El Sauzal (➤ 77). Follow the signs to the **❻ Casa del Vino La Baranda** (➤ 77), a wine museum in a fine old restored *hacienda*. Here you can learn about the island's wine-growing history and enjoy a tasty lunch over a delicious local tipple.

4:00pm

After lunch, proceed to **❻ El Sauzal** (➤ 77) for a quick look around, then drive back to Tacoronte before going north towards the town of Valle de Guerra. Shortly before you reach it, you can stop to visit another beautiful country house, the **❼ Casa de Carta** (top right; ➤ 78), home to the Museo de Antropología (Anthropology Museum).

5:30pm
Before returning to La Laguna for the evening, you could continue up the road to **8 Bajamar** (below; ➤ 78) and **Punta del Hidalgo** further on (➤ 78), two rocky, black-sand coastal resorts. Take an evening swim in the water pools, have a sunset drink and then drive back to La Laguna (16km/10 miles) for dinner (➤ 79).

Day Two

The second day takes you around the **2 Montañas de Anaga** (➤ 73). The options are broad, but it is worth visiting the towns of **Taganana** (➤ 73), **Taborno** (➤ 74) and **Chinamada** (➤ 74), as well as the **beaches**, where the seafood restaurants of **Playa de San Roque** make a good lunch stop. Try the suggested driving route (➤ 160–162).

❶ La Laguna

Properly known as San Cristóbal de la Laguna, the original town rose next to a small lake. As well as being the capital, La Laguna was the Canary Islands' military headquarters and, since 1819, has been the seat of the Nivariense diocese (*Nivaria* was the island's ancient Latin name), which covers Tenerife and the other western islands. With more than 100,000 inhabitants, it is also an important university centre. The old town, with its imposing churches, convents and mansions, is a joy to explore.

The leafy **Plaza del Adelantado**, fronted by the baroque (but much revamped) *ayuntamiento* (town hall) and the busy produce market, is a good place to start exploring the old town. Behind the town hall on **Calle Obispo Rey Redondo** is the sumptuous 17th-century **Casa de los Capitanes**, originally the residence of the island's military commanders and now used for temporary art exhibitions.

Religious Buildings
The **Catedral**, with a neoclassical facade, was rebuilt in 1913 in neo-Gothic style. Among its artistic treasures are the 18th-century pulpit, as well as the **Retablo de los Remedios**, which depicts Biblical allegories and several miracles. Its creator was Martín de Vos, a 16th-century student of one of the Great Renaissance Masters, Tintoretto.

More emblematic of the religious importance of La Laguna is the **Iglesia de la Concepción**, whose belfry is known simply as La Torre (The Tower). Although much tampered with since it was first built in the early 16th century, the

The Plaza de San Francisco in La Laguna

The neo-classical facade of the Catedral obscures a neo-Gothic interior

church still has traces of its late Gothic origins. Inside, the faithful are protected from the elements by two fine *mudéjar* timber ceilings. Two of the Canary Islands' most important pre-19th-century artists, Cristóbal Hernández de Quintana (1659–1725) and Juan de Miranda (1723–1805), both left paintings here. Several important religious orders established convents and monasteries in La Laguna, among the most important being the **Convento de Santa Clara**, on Calle Nava y Grimón. The convent's church has an admirable timber ceiling, but it is closed while restoration work is carried out.

Grand Old Houses

More interesting for some will be La Laguna's graceful **Canary Island mansions**. Never rising more than three floors, they stand out above all for the extensive use of timber, especially in the ornate doors and heavily framed sash windows. Behind the facades are lovely interior *patios* (courtyards). Keep a look out for open doors into these grand old houses, as frequently you can go inside far enough to see the courtyards.

Some of the most important of these houses can be seen on **Calle San Agustín**. No 28, **Casa Salazar**, is in fact the bishop's residence, but during working hours you can usually go in to admire the *patio*. Just down the road at No 16 is the **Casa Montañés**, built in the 17th century, with fine timber work in the doors, windows and courtyards.

The pick of the crop is Casa Lercaro, between the two. It has been converted into the **Museo de Historia y Antropología de Tenerife**, which is interesting in itself, but a visit is also worthwhile just to inspect the house. The outstanding feature is the polished timber, used in everything from the ceilings to the floors. The museum displays are in Spanish, but they allow you to get a handle on the pre-Spanish history of Tenerife, its conquest and developments up to the present. On show are documents, maps and explanatory panels as well as artefacts, tools and household items ranging through the centuries.

TAKING A BREAK
Take a load off and enjoy a soothing ale at one of the terrazas on **Plaza del Adelantado**. Or splash out on a good meal at the nearby **El Principito** restaurant (Calle de Santo Domingo 26, tel: 922/633-916, moderate) which offers French and Spanish dishes, with fish specialities.

Museo de la
Ciencia y el
Cosmos

➕ 181 D4

Catedral
✉ Plaza de la Catedral s/n 🕐 Closed
for refurbishment

Iglesia de la Concepción
✉ Plaza de la Concepción s/n 🕐 Daily
9–1:30, 6–8:30

**Museo de Historia y Antropología
de Tenerife**
✉ Calle San Agustín 22 ☎ 922/825-
949 🕐 Tue–Sun 9–7 💶 Moderate,
Sun free

Museo de la Ciencia y el Cosmos
✉ Calle Vía Láctea s/n ☎ 922/315-265
🕐 Tue–Sun 9–7 💶 Moderate, Sun free

Real Santuario del Santísimo Cristo
✉ Plaza de San Francisco s/n
🕐 Mon–Sat 9–1, 4–9; Sun 9–9 💶 Free

LA LAGUNA: INSIDE INFO

Top tips The 16th-century **Real Santuario del Santísimo Cristo** (Royal Sanctuary of the Most Holy Christ), also known as the Santuario de San Francisco church, is home to a black Gothic wooden sculpture of Christ.
■ La Laguna is now linked to downtown Santa Cruz by tram (➤ 33).

In more depth You might want to check out the **Museo de la Ciencia y el Cosmos**, a little way out of the centre of town (pictured above). An interactive science museum, it is popular with kids. The emphasis is on astronomy (including a planetarium), which is hardly surprising given the important telescope observatories on Tenerife and La Palma, whose activities are co-ordinated by the Instituto de Astrofísica de Canarias (IAC) at La Laguna University (➤ box, 120).

2 Montañas de Anaga

The rugged Anaga mountain range that dominates the northeast corner of Tenerife is a nature reserve and an escape for the citizens of La Laguna and Santa Cruz. Aware of their importance in the face of the barely contained urban sprawl of the cities, Tinerfeños are making sure that no harm comes to the Anaga, part of which is a protected park. You can drive along narrow winding roads to small villages or, better still, put on your hiking boots and follow the trails that, in some cases, bring you out to impressive points along the island's wild northeast coast.

Around Taganana

The village of Las Mercedes sits on the steep Anaga hillside

The most substantial Anaga town is **Taganana**. It slithers down a steep hillside facing the ocean on the northern flank of the Anaga. About halfway down the slope is the **Iglesia de Nuestra Señora de las Nieves**, known mainly for a 16th-century Flemish triptych (quite a way from its original home),

WALKING THE ROYAL WAY

Long before asphalt roads, the Montañas de Anaga were criss-crossed by a series of narrow trails known as *caminos reales* (royal ways). Several of these still exist and make for great walking opportunities. Among the best known is the **Vueltas de Taganana**, which snakes its way from the main TF12 highway (the trail starts at a *casa forestal* – forest ranger's hut) across the Llano de las Vueltas (Vueltas Plain) north to Taganana. It takes about 1.5 hours to reach Taganana, and you can walk back by following a driving track via a settlement west of Taganana called Las Chozas (the full duration is about three hours). You will pass through thick woods and be rewarded along the way with some really stunning views of the north coast.

and a cheerful square. In terms of monuments there is not much else to it, but the precarious lanes lined with humble houses transport you into another world and there are fine views of the coast and the palm-laden *barranco* (gorge).

Further West

Another intriguing hamlet is **Taborno**, with its scattering of houses along a ridge jutting north. The views from the top of the village out over the coast are breathtaking.

To the north is the **Roque de Taborno** (706m/2,316 feet), a rocky outcrop shaped a bit like an artillery shell and covered in trees.

A little harder to get to is the remarkable hamlet of **Chinamada**. About halfway down the TF145, which drops north from the TF12 towards Las Carboneras, a 5km (3-mile) walking trail to Chinamada is signposted. It takes about three hours to get there and back, with a little time thrown in to look around.

The cave houses of Chinamada are worth the time it takes to hike to them

Apart from the sense of isolation, the main point of interest are the *cave houses*, partly built into the rock. Only a handful of people live in these semi-troglodyte dwellings, and surprisingly their interiors are much like those of any modern house. The walking trail continues for about an hour northwest to **Punta del Hidalgo** (➤ 78) on the coast.

To the East

On the eastern side of the Anaga range, the road peters out in the village of **Chamorga**. It is as much

The Anaga coast offers good conditions for surfers

the driving route around here (➤ 160–162) as the place itself that is of interest. Aside from a small chapel, higgledy-piggledy houses and some dragon trees, there is little to this half-abandoned farming village. However, it does offer several walking possibilities and the starting point for several trails is signposted. The most popular takes you to **Roque Bermejo**, a tiny settlement (with nearby lighthouse) on the east coast.

The coast also offers some surprises. **Surfers** come to the black-sand beaches off the north Anaga coast to catch waves – the swell here is about the best on Tenerife for surfing.

For a quieter seaside experience you could make for **Playa de Antequera**, south of the mountains and about 4km (2.5 miles) east of Igueste (➤ 56) – an hour's walk. Locals often turn up by boat, easily the most relaxing method of approach.

If you happen to be in the Anaga Mountains on a clear day, there are some fine **lookout points** to aim for, including, from east to west, the Mirador del Bailadero, the Mirador del Pico del Inglés and the Mirador de la Cruz del Carmen.

TAKING A BREAK

There are several simple **fish restaurants** lined up opposite Playa de San Roque. Just take your pick!

Chinamada ➕ 181 D5
Playa de San Roque ➕ 181 E5
Taganana ➕ 181 E5
Taborno ➕ 181 D5

MONTAÑAS DE ANAGA: INSIDE INFO

Top tip Hikers should bear several things in mind in the Anaga Mountains. Always carry sufficient **food and water** as in many of the small villages you cannot count on finding even a shop open. Wear **good hiking boots** and **be prepared** for all seasons. A hot, sunny morning can quickly turn into a squally afternoon, with mist, rain and biting winds.

At Your Leisure

❸ Stunt Galería de Arte

This small gallery is one of the leading contemporary art organisations on the island with a regular exhibition programme featuring local and mainland Spanish artists supplemented with works by foreign artists.

✚ 181 D4 ✉ Calle Bencomo 7, La Laguna
☎ 922/252-528; www.stunt.es

❹ Bosque de la Esperanza

The thick woods of the Bosque de la Esperanza cover a high ridge that climbs southwest from La Laguna towards Mount Teide (➤ 118–122) and forms part of the island's volcanic backbone. The woods are wonderful for walking and along the road that runs through the middle are scattered eight fine *miradores* (lookout points).

If you are driving from La Laguna, take the TF24 road towards the unremarkable town of La Esperanza. The real treat begins as you gain altitude and enter the forest itself,

The summit of Mount Teide can be seen across a sea of clouds from the Bosque de la Esperanza

filled with laurels and other species of trees. Marked trails fall away from either side of the ridge, which the road follows through the length of the forest and beyond towards Mount Teide. Among the better lookouts to stop at are the **Mirador Pico de las Flores**, from where you can gaze north to La Laguna and beyond to the Anaga Mountains, and the **Mirador de Ortuño** (10km/6 miles further), where you get the first good look at Mount Teide. The best is about 2km (1 mile) on, where a lane branches right off the main road to the **Mirador de las Cumbres**. The views of Mount Teide from here are impressive, as are those of the forest. About 10km (6 miles) further on you emerge from the forest into the stark landscape around Mount Teide.

✚ 180 B3 ✉ 5km (3 miles) south of La Laguna

5 Tacoronte

Tacoronte lies at the heart of Tenerife's wine country. It is a pleasant town and worth a stop while on an unhurried tour of the area. The name Tacoronte is believed to be a Guanche word meaning "the place where the elders meet", leading archaeologists to suggest that it was a capital for one of the Guanche tribes. After the Spanish conquest of the islands it received a community of Portuguese settlers.

The old nucleus of the town gathers around the **Iglesia del Cristo de los Dolores** (Church of the Sorrows of Christ) and the nearby **Iglesia de Santa Catalina**.

The former houses a much-venerated 17th-century image of Christ (the church is also known as the Santuario del Santísimo Cristo – Sanctuary of the Most Holy Christ). Construction on the Iglesia de Santa Catalina started in the early 16th century, but it wasn't finished until towards the end of the 18th century. Inside is a charming *artesonado* ceiling (a timber ceiling divided into squares into which wooden inserts, or *artesas*, with some kind of motif, are placed). Around the two churches gathers a web of tight lanes and several townhouses.

Tacoronte can get lively, especially in the Fiestas de la Vendimia (Grape Harvest Festival) during September.

🔠 180 B4 ✉ 9km (5.5 miles) west of La Laguna

Palm trees and pot plants adorn El Sauzal's town hall

6 El Sauzal and Casa del Vino la Baranda

Just by the motorway exit for El Sauzal stands a 17th-century *hacienda* (farm) now used as a wine showcase and museum for Tenerife, the **Casa del Vino la Baranda**. The house, founded by a merchant originally from Andalucía in southern Spain, was the nucleus of a sprawling property that, for a few years, during the mid-19th century passed into the hands of the President of Mexico, José Joaquín de Herrera.

Originally known as the Quinta de San Simón del Sauzal, the house was taken over and restored by the Tenerife government in 1992 and converted into the attractive wine museum it is today.

After entering you pass through reception on the left and into what was the founder's family chapel, notable for the original (unrestored) *artesonado* ceiling. Down the hall are exhibition rooms and, at the end, a tasteful bar and restaurant area. Across the courtyard is the museum, a well-presented exploration of the history of Tenerife's wines and their growers. Attached to the museum is an enticing wine shop and wine-tasting room. On summer evenings you can catch classical music concerts on the *patio*.

El Sauzal itself is a pleasant place, filled with well-appointed and attractive villas, and enticing small restaurants. In the centre is the unusual **Iglesia de San Pedro**, notable for its whitewashed Moorish-looking dome. Make for the **Mirador**

de la Garañona, a marvellous lookout with views out over the cliff walls.
➕ 180 B4

Casa del Vino La Baranda
✉ Autopista General del Norte, Km 21
☎ 922/572-535; www.tenerife.es/casa-vino
🕐 Apr–Oct Wed–Sat 10–9:30; Sun 11–6; Tue 11:30–7:30, Nov–Mar Tue, Wed–Sat 10–9:30; Sun 11–6; 10:30–6:30 💲 Free

7 Casa de Carta (Museo de Antropología)

A detour north from Tacoronte towards the hamlet of Valle de Guerra leads you to this beautiful country home now turned into the **Museo de Antropología** (Anthropology Museum). This is the kind of museum you can visit more than once, because they keep changing the exhibitions. The themes are varied but always include an element linked with the culture and past of the islands, ranging from cuisine to Guanche traditions.
➕ 180 B4 ✉ Tacoronte– Valle de Guerra road ☎ 922/546-300; www.museosdetenerife. org 🕐 Tue–Sun 9–7 💲 Free

8 Bajamar and Punta del Hidalgo

These two coastal towns, only 4km (2.5 miles) apart, form a dated

An unexpected skyscraper on the headland near Punta del Hidalgo

coastal resort on the north flank of the Anaga Mountains. Although due for a major facelift as it is full of unattractive apartments and soulless hotels, the two resorts are relaxed and the landscape around them impressive. Waves pound the black volcanic rock – apart from the modest black strand at **Bajamar** (meaning "down by the sea") there is nothing in the way of beaches here – against the majestic background of the Anaga Mountains.

The road ends with **Punta del Hidalgo** – the only way to continue from here is on foot. The most curious items are the *piscinas naturales*, the "natural pools" that have been carved out of the rock. On a stormy day you can find yourself in mid lap, only to have waves crash over the barriers and into the tranquillity of the pool. Indeed, this is a windy corner, with gusts whipping up the ocean.

It's unlikely that either resort will attract you enough to stay, but it's worth dropping by for a swim and to have a look around.
➕ 180 C5 ✉ Bajamar 8km (5 miles) north of La Laguna ✉ Punta del Hidalgo 11km (7 miles) north of La Laguna

Where to...
Stay

Prices
The following price ranges are for a double room in high season, IGIC sales tax included. Rates vary seasonally.

€ under €70   €€ €70–€120   €€€ over €120

BAJAMAR

Hotel Delfin Bajamar €
If you want a cosy budget hotel close to the water in Tenerife's wild coastal region with walking and hiking on the doorstep, you have it here. The Hotel Delfin Bajamar is only 25m (27 yeards) away from the white-sand beach and it is a low-key 3-star property set in the village overlooking the man-made pools and the surrounding cliffs. It looks rather boxy from the outside, but the rooms, set on five floors are bright and airy.

There's a fresh-water swimming pool, tennis court and solarium on site. One floor has rooms adapted for disabled guests.
✚ 180 C5 ⊠ Avenida del Sol 39, Bajamar ☎ 922/540-200; www.delfinbajamar.com

LA LAGUNA

Aguere €
This delightful B&B in the old quarter is a completely "non-package" experience. The 18th-century house was once a bishop's palace and has 22 rooms rambling around the skylit upper gallery. It was later used as school accommodation but was converted into a hotel in 1885. The 22 rooms of varying size have been refurbished and are airy and spacious. Breakfast is included in the price and is the only meal served. Take it under the swaying palms in the courtyard.
✚ 181 D4 ⊠ Calle La Carrera 55 ☎ 922/259-490; www.hotelaguere.es

Hotel-Apartamentos Nivaria €€
Set on the south side of La Lagunas charming central old town square, this 18th-century building has kept something of its original character despite being modernised. An elegant *patio* is one of its prime feature, and the interior, if rather sombre in parts, has an authentic Spanish atmosphere.

The 73 rooms include studios for two and apartments for up to three, furnished in modern and traditional styles. There is a restaurant and a café-bar on site, and a squash court is an unexpected plus point.

Guests can also take advantage of the complimentary internet access or bicycles.
✚ 181 D4 ⊠ Plaza del Adelantado 11 ☎ 922/264-298; www.hotelnivaria.com

TACORONTE

El Adelantado €
A large traditional 18th-century farmhouse in ample grounds in the heart of the north can be rented per room or as a large villa. The house has two cosy sitting rooms and a room where breakfast is served. There's a terrace overlooking the private vineyard: the estate is on north-facing slopes at an altitude of more than 500m (1,600 feet) and is in one of the most important wine-growing areas on the island. The owners run bonsai workshops and have have gardens specialising in Canarian plants. There's a minimum stay of three nights.
✚ 180 B4 ⊠ El Alentado 16, Tacoronte ☎ 922/271-135; www.casaruraleladelantado.com

Where to...
Eat and Drink

Prices

The following price ranges indicate what you can expect to pay per person for a meal, including drinks, tax and tip.

€ under €18   **€€** €18–€36   **€€€** over €36

Some excellent family restaurants are located on the country roads around La Esperanza and the Anaga Mountains. Many restaurants have a strong local ambience, in contrast to the more touristy places found in the international resorts. A lively bar and café scene centres on La Laguna's university quarter, especially around Plaza Zurita. The area is known as El Cuadrilátero and teems with around 60 bars. Thousands of students revel in spots like the the Irish-style Cerveceria 7 Islas (Calle Heraclio Sanchez) for its choice beers and, El Buho (Calle Catedral 3) and Pub Harina (Calle Dr Zamenhof 9).

LA LAGUNA

Asador Neke €–€€

This restaurant has grown from a simple BBQ place into an expansive eatery on the back of a good reputation for well-cooked dishes using the best ingredients, many locally sourced. There's a pretty dining room and terrace with starched tablecloths that hints at attention to detail. The menu offers a good range of meats, seafood and salad dishes.

⊞ 181 D4 **⊠** Subida del Pulpito, close to the Aeropuerto del Norte **☎** 922/257-166 **⊙** Mon–Sat noon–4, 8–midnight

Patio Canario €–€€

While perhaps nudging the touristy, the courtyard after which this Canarian eatery is named is a pleasant setting for tapas, cheese and meat platters, and other goodies. It is set in an 18th-century house and the *patio* in question is preceded by a friendly bar area.

⊞ 181 D4 **⊠** Calle Manuel de Ossuna 8 **☎** 922/264-657 **⊙** Mon–Sat noon–4:30, 8–1am

El Tonique €–€€

Dine in a cellar-style dining room in wood, brick and stone, with walls partly lined with a selection of its 150 varieties of wine. The mainstay of this wine bar's menu consists of imaginative, generously sized tapas, but main courses are also available. This place is popular with a lively young local crowd as well as business people.

⊞ 181 D4 **⊠** Calle Heraclio Sánchez 23 **☎** 922/261-529 **⊙** Mon 8pm–12:30am, Tue–Sat 1–4:30, 8–12:30; closed 15–30 Aug

TACORONTE

Los Limoneros €€€

This elegant, formal restaurant lies in a quiet, rural spot just east of the village of Los Naranjeros, providing a civilised setting for its well-heeled clientele. It's also a restaurant frequented by the Spanish royal family when they visit Tenerife. You will find mostly business folk during the week, although families flock here in droves for huge feasts at the weekends. The cooking is traditional, making much use of lamb and fish, and service is generally courteous.

⊞ 180 B4 **⊠** Carretera General del Norte 447B Km15.5 **☎** 922/636-637 **⊙** Mon–Sat 1pm–midnight

Mi Merced €–€€

This lovely interior is a typical formal Spanish café with a highly polished mahogany bar and marble floor. The food is also classical in style with both Canarian and Castilian choices as well as excellent grilled meats.

➕ 180 B4 ⊠ Camino Real 280, Barranco las Lajas ☎ 922/567-236 ⏰ Wed–Sat noon–5pm, 8–10:30; Sun noon–5pm. Closed Mon and Tue

EL SAUZAL

Casa del Vino La Baranda €€

The tapas-bar and restaurant attached to the wine museum (▶ 77) gives visitors a chance to sample some of the island's best wine produce before buying it to take away. The lovely 17th-century country house has an elegantly atmospheric setting, the Canarian dishes are well prepared and tasty, and there's an increasingly cheerful buzz as glasses are raised.

➕ 180 B4 ⊠ El Sauzal ☎ 922/563-886 ⏰ Tue–Sat 1–4, 8–11, Sun 1–4

Restaurante Martínez €–€€

Brimming plates of typical Castilian cuisine plus an ample choice of tapas are the staple offerings of this rustic wine bar where you can enjoy local wines by the carafe with your choice of food. Traditional *bacalao* (salted cod) is a local favourite but there is a good range of fish and meat grilled to your liking.

➕ 180 B4 ⊠ Carretera General del Norte 119 ☎ 922/564-044; www.restaurantemartinez.com ⏰ Sat–Tue, Thu 9:30–4; Fri 9:30–4, 7–11. Closed Wed

TEGUESTE

El Drago €€€

El Drago is a charming old farmhouse producing classic Canarian cooking. Specialities include *sopa de puerros con queso fresco* (leek soup with soft cheese) or *cabrito asado con papas negras* (roast kid with black potatoes).

➕ 180 C4 ⊠ Calle Marqués de Celada 2 ☎ 922/543-001 ⏰ Fri–Sat 1–4, 8–11, Wed–Thu, Sun 1–4; closed Aug

Where to...
Shop

SOUVENIRS

This area isn't really geared towards tourist shopping, although there are a few shops within La Laguna's old quarter. **Casa de los Calados** (Calle Núñez de la Peña 9) sells embroidery while **Atlantida Artesanía** (Calle San Agustín 55) sells a range of island products. A covered **produce market** (Mon–Sat morning) is held on Calle San Agustín near Plaza del Adelantado.

WINE

The Tacoronte region is famed for its wines and a great place to buy is the **Casa del Vino La Baranda** (▶ 77) at El Sauzal. For a small fee, you can taste wines, and get advice from the knowledgeable, multilingual staff in the impressive shop/wine museum. Another good place is **Bodega Alvaro** (2km/1.2 miles outside Tacoronte on the La Laguna road, tel: 922/ 560-359; Mon–Sat 9–5:30). Tenerife's largest wine dealer.

WALKING MAPS

If you're planning to explore the Anaga Mountains in the northeast in any detail, make sure you invest in a decent map before setting off. A selection of **walking maps and guides** is available either at La Laguna's information office on Plaza del Adelantado (▶ 70), or at the Mirador Cruz del Carmen visitor centre (▶ 82).

Where to...
Be Entertained

LA LAGUNA

Entertainment in La Laguna caters mainly for locals and students. Concerts, art exhibitions, arthouse films and theatre productions tend to be more highbrow than in other parts of the island, and virtually all performances will be in Spanish.

The city comes to life during its annual **jazz and international theatre festivals**. During Corpus Cristi (May–June), elaborate carpets of coloured sand and flowers are created in the streets, and visitors flock in from all the local islands. If you have children to amuse on a wet day, try La Laguna's **Museo de la Ciencia y el Cosmos** (Vía Láctea, tel: 922/315-265; Tue–Sun 9–7, moderate), a space and science museum with hands-on activities.

WALKING AND HIKING

Most visitors go to the northeast for exhilarating scenery and fresh air. The few roads through the Anaga Mountains can get congested in high season (watch out for stray goats on the bends). Plan walks carefully as few routes form easy round-trips, and there's no accommodation in the mountains. Though altitudes are moderate, gradients are steep and weather conditions can change quickly.

Footpaths meander all over this steeply contoured peninsula. For maps and route information, visit the Anaga Park information centre at **Cruz del Carmen** (tel: 922/633-576), where there's a panoramic *mirador* and a simple restaurant. Its a good starting point for splendid walks through primeval **laurel forest** to pretty villages like Las Carboneras or El Batán. Other interesting routes can be followed from Chamorga or round the rugged coastline from Taganana. The driveable road ends at Benijo, but paths lead to the lighthouse (Faro de Anaga).

BIRDWATCHING

Keen birdwatchers should keep an eye open for one of Tenerife's unique endemic species, **Bolle's Pigeon**. You may be lucky enough to see it perching on branches in the laurel forests of the Anaga Mountains. **Punta del Hidalgo** (▶ 78) is a good place to spot spring migrants.

Find somewhere safe to stop and listen out for **native canaries** singing along the wooded roadsides between Las Mercedes and La Laguna. The dense pine forests of **La Esperanza** may give tantalising glimpses of Tenerife's tiny acrobatic goldcrest, and also the beautiful blue chaffinch. A good place to see them is from the *mirador* at El Diablillo on the Cumbre Dorsal from Esperanza to Mount Teide.

WATERSPORTS

The coves east of the **Punta del Hidalgo** (▶ 78) and big waves whipped up by onshore winds attract **surfers**. But the currents round the northern cape can be dangerous, so you need to be more advanced than a beginner here. A safer place to **swim** is the low-key resort of **Bajamar** (▶ 78), where you can bathe in tidal rock pools surrounded by protective reefs.

GOLF

The smartest of Tenerife's courses is the **Real Club de Golf de Tenerife** near Tacoronte (tel: 922/636-607; www.realclubgolftenerife.com). Its rolling fairways offer a splendid view of Mount Teide.

The Northwest

Getting Your Bearings

The western half of Tenerife's northern coastal strip is the area of the island richest in interest for visitors, with historical town centres, a comparatively low-key seaside resort, fishing villages, strange trees, rugged coast, banana plantations, an interactive zoo and the rugged mountain terrain around the village of Masca at the head of a gorge.

Although long dedicated to the business of tourism, Puerto de la Cruz is an interesting coastal town that has managed to preserve much of the charm of its old centre. More engaging still is the inland town of La Orotava, the prettiest old colonial

Page 83: Walls of volcanic rocks at Acantilado de los Gigantes

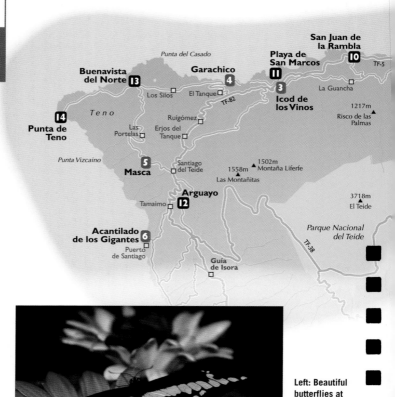

San Juan de la Rambla 10

Punta del Casado

Playa de San Marcos 11

Garachico 4

TF-5

Buenavista del Norte 13

Los Silos El Tanque

La Guancha

Icod de los Vinos

TF-82

Teno

Ruigómez

Icod de los Vinos 3

1217m Risco de las Palmas

14 Punta de Teno

Las Portelas Erjos del Tanque

Punta Vizcaino

5 Masca

Santiago del Teide

1502m Montaña Liferfe 1558m Las Montañitas

3718m El Teide

Arguayo 12

Tamaimo

Parque Nacional del Teide

Acantilado de los Gigantes 6

Puerto de Santiago

Guía de Isora

TF-38

Left: Beautiful butterflies at Icod de los Vinos

Puerto
de la Cruz

Loro
Parque **7**

Bananera
El Guanche
8

Los Realejos **9** TF-5 **1** La Orotava
Cruz
Santa   **Pueblo
Chico**
Valle de la Orotava   Aguamansa

★ **Don't Miss**

At Your Leisure

**Above: La
Orotava is a
pretty colonial
town**

city in the Canary Islands and set in one of Tenerife's most
attractive valleys.

A series of beaches and villages reveals itself as you head
west. Marvel at the ancient dragon tree and exotic butterflies
in Icod de los Vinos, lie on the nearby beach at San Marcos,
explore the fishing hamlet of Garachico, or opt to drive away
from it all to Punta de Teno, which juts arrogantly into the
Atlantic at the island's westernmost point.

The majesty of the coast is matched by the abruptness
of its hinterland, which rears up to the east. An unequalled
vantage point from which to enjoy a Tenerife sunset is the
pretty mountain hamlet of Masca, along whose gorge you
can also trek to the coast.

In Three Days

If you're not quite sure where to begin your travels, this itinerary recommends three practical and enjoyable days out in the Northwest, taking in some of the best places to see using the Getting Your Bearings map on the previous page. For more information see the main entries.

Day One

Morning

Plan to arrive in **❶ La Orotava** (Jardines Marquesado de la Quinta Roja, right; ➤ 88–92) in the morning. Go on a walking tour of the town, which is full of wonderful old Canarian houses. Don't miss the Casas de los Balcones, the Museo de Artesanía Iberoamericana and the baroque Iglesia de Nuestra Señora de la Concepción. Next head down to **❷ Puerto de la Cruz** (➤ 93–95), a short drive or bus/taxi ride. Stop at **❽ Bananera El Guanche** (➤ 104) for a quick inspection of the banana trees and other exotic flora before reaching Puerto de la Cruz itself. Then make for the **Casa de Miranda** (➤ 94), an 18th-century mansion by the sea in the heart of town, for lunch.

Afternoon

Several choices present themselves. You could soak up some sun at **Lago Martiánez** or **Playa Jardín** (➤ 93), visit the island's popular zoo, **❼ Loro Parque** (above; ➤ 104), or simply explore the town on foot. You can easily combine two of these. There are plenty of dining options in Puerto de la Cruz (➤ 109–110) before returning to La Orotava for the night.

Day Two

Morning

Take the highway west towards **3 Icod de los Vinos** (►96–97). The top of everyone's list is the **Drago Milenario** (Thousand-Year-Old Dragon Tree; right). Take time for a leisurely stroll about the town centre and consider a visit to the **Mariposario del Drago** (Butterfly Museum, ►97). Drive the few kilometres down to Icod's local beach, **11 Playa de San Marcos** (►105), where you can enjoy a swim in the protected bay and indulge in lunch at one of the waterfront restaurants.

Afternoon

From Playa de San Marcos it is 7km (4.5 miles) to **4 Garachico** (►98–99), a charming fishing town that was once also one of Tenerife's senior ports. There is plenty to occupy an afternoon, from the natural ocean pools to the former Convento de San Francisco.

Day Three

Follow the circular driving tour (►163–166). If you devoted the previous morning to Icod de los Vinos, you can drive straight through and, in a further variation from the suggested route, duck south to see the **6 Acantilado de los Gigantes** cliffs (►102–103) before backtracking to **5 Masca** (►100–101). From there you will head to **14 Punta de Teno** (►106) and possibly stop outside **13 Buenavista del Norte** for dinner before returning to Garachico for the night.

❶ La Orotava

Already in the times of the Guanches, the Valle de la Orotava (Orotava Valley) was considered one of the richest areas in Tenerife. Spanish settlers were quick to move in and the valley remains a luxuriant farming oasis. The town of La Orotava, with the best-preserved historical centre in the archipelago, really took off in the 18th century when important families from La Laguna moved in and used their wine wealth to build fine mansions and churches.

The streets of old La Orotava constitute a virtual open-air museum of the Canary Islands' domestic architecture. Most of the houses that huddle together along the steep streets date from the 17th and 18th centuries.

You may have already seen grand **Canary Island colonial houses**, whether old or relatively new, in places like La Laguna or Puerto de la Cruz, but they pale before their more ambitious cousins in La Orotava. Take the **Casas de los Balcones** on Calle San Francisco, without doubt the stars of the show. As you approach uphill, you cannot help but be impressed by

The snow-capped peak of Mount Teide rears behind the island's north coast

the heavy teak balconies that line the length of two adjoining houses, the 17th-century Casa Fonseca and 17th- to 18th-century Casa Franchi.

18th-century Style

Inside the **Casa Fonseca**, which was once the home of a notable family and today houses a shop selling arts and crafts, you get an idea of how the other half lived during the heyday of Tenerife's wine boom. Through the shop you pass into the rear courtyards. Filled with plants and palms, and with a huge wine-press at the rear, the *patio* is surmounted by elegant enclosed galleries on the first floor.

Well-kept and colourful houses brighten up the town's streets

Upstairs is a museum, basically the family home decked out in 18th-century style. Climb the spiral staircase to explore the salon, bedrooms, dining room, traditional kitchen, galleries and corridors.

The workshops produce traditional goods of a high quality and the whole centre is designed to keep alive the traditions of the island. The colourful **Romería de San Isidro Labrador y Santa María de la Cabeza** (the Sunday after Corpus Cristi in May–June, ➤ 10) starts from here.

Next door, the **Casa Franchi** is less spectacular inside. You can usually enter the atrium to view the *patio*, which is smaller

and darker than the one in the Casa Fonseca.

Across the road is a third house, the so-called **Casa del Turista**, which dates to 1590 and traditionally is known as the **Casa Molina**. It is basically another enormous stockpile of every conceivable type of crafts, including ceramics, embroidery (for which the island has a strong reputation) and other objects. The staff wander around in traditional dress.

At the back is a *patio* with a difference, for instead of being closed in on all sides, it is open at the rear, allowing splendid views to Puerto de la Cruz and out to sea. On permanent display here is a "carpet" made of different coloured volcanic sands. As part of the Corpus Cristi celebrations in June (➤ 10), the people of La Orotava have been weaving these carpets since the mid-19th century.

Architectural detail from a disused *gofio* mill in La Orotava

Gofio

A few paces uphill in the triangular **Plaza San Francisco** stand the remains of a *gofio* **mill**. If you develop a hankering to see more decommissioned mills, you could continue along Calle Doctor Domingo González García and, in the space of about 0.5km (0.3 miles), you can see half a dozen such mills in varying states of disrepair. If you want to see a mill in action, head downhill about 100m (110 yards) from the Casas de los Balcones and there is a working mill on the left in Calle Colegio. The building survives from the 17th century and below you can still see the aqueduct that fed the original water-driven mill. Today it runs on electricity. If you wish to try the floury powder that has long been the main staple in the islanders' diet (➤ panel below), this is the place to do it.

Crafts

More crafts are on display in the **Museo de Artesanía Iberoamericana**. Housed in the exquisite cloister of the

---

GULPING DOWN YOUR *GOFIO*

In Guanche times the staple food was a powder called *gofio*, a toasted and finely ground cereal used to make all sorts of things. It is now most commonly made of wheat or corn, but other cereals like barley can be used. In its various versions it has the consistency of flour. Islanders swear that globs of the stuff drenched in milk make the perfect healthy breakfast and other recipes range from tortilla with a *gofio* base to biscuits of baked *gofio* and honey. *Gofio* took root in some parts of South America but mainland Spaniards never acquired the taste – so you can find it in Miami but not Madrid!

former convent of the Iglesia de Santo Domingo (the church rarely opens except for Mass – your best bet is from about 4:30–7pm), it contains two floors of wide-ranging arts and crafts from all over Spain, Portugal and South America.

The ground floor is roughly divided into two parts, one devoted to musical instruments and the other to ceramics. The instruments range from Cuban papier-mâché maracas to a bamboo violin from Colombia or the *charango*, a Bolivian string instrument made from an armadillo hide. Examples of ceramics from various South American countries and almost every Spanish region are on display, among them items from traditional centres such as Talavera de la Reina, Toledo and Paterna (in Valencia).

Upstairs the mix of items is greater still. Everything from a canoe made of reeds to bizarre, candelabras and trees of life from Mexico fill the rooms. All sorts of textiles, several more musical instruments and indigenous art from across South America complete the picture.

A quick trip to church might be in order to counteract the overwhelming amount of crafts on offer in La Orotava. The **Iglesia de Nuestra Señora de la Concepción** is a masterpiece of baroque architecture and doubtless the most important example throughout the islands. It is flanked by two towers and topped by an imposing dome. The facade, it is said, symbolises the close relationship between the Canaries and South America. The main altar is graced by a marble and alabaster tabernacle.

TAKING A BREAK

The baroque
Iglesia de
Nuestra
Señora de la
Concepción

Stop for refreshment on **Plaza de la Constitución** or for a full meal there's the **Sabor Canario** in the heart of the old town (► 109). This restaurant is nicely situated on the *patio* of a typical old La Orotava house. Shoppers can browse in the attached arts and crafts store. Another attractive option is the nearby **Casa Lercaro**, yet another fine example of a rambling Canarian mansion where you can both dine and shop (► 109).

✚ 180 A3

Casas de los Balcones
✉ Calle San Francisco 3
☎ 922/330-629,
www.casa-balcones.com
🕙 Mon–Sat 8:30–6:30
💷 Inexpensive

Casa del Turista
✉ Calle San Francisco 4
☎ 922/330-629 🕙 Mon–Sat 8:30–

7:30, Sun 8:30–1:30 💷 Free

Museo de Artesanía
Iberoamericana
✉ Calle Tomás Zerolo 34
☎ 922/323-376 🕙 Mon 9–3,
Tue–Fri 9–5, Sat 9–1. Closed Sun
💷 Moderate

Iglesia de la Concepción
✉ Plaza Casañas 🕙 Daily 9–1,
4:30–8 💷 Free

LA OROTAVA: INSIDE INFO

Top tips Pottery lovers should visit the **Museo de Cerámica** (Calle Leon 3, tel: 922/321-447, Mon–Sat 10–6, Sun 10–2, inexpensive; pictured above) in the Casa Tafuriaste. The museum is upstairs in this restored house, or you could just wander around the extensive showroom situated on the ground floor.

■ Presiding high over Plaza de la Constitución is the **Liceo de Taoro** (tel: 922/330-119, www.liceotaoro.com, daily 9am–midnight, inexpensive), a luxury club where, for a modest fee, you can become a day member and have a drink. There are occasional art expos and cultural events too.

■ Next door to the Liceo de Taoro are the pleasant gardens, **Jardines Marquesado de la Quinta Roja** (Calle San Agustín, daily 9–6, free).

■ Another charming little garden is the **Hijuela del Bótanico** (Calle Tomás Pérez, Mon–Fri 9–2, free), a mini-botanical collection on Calle Tomás Pérez .

Hidden gem You might easily walk past the **Casa Torrehermosa** (Mon–Fri 9:30–4, Sat 9–1; free; www.artenerife.com), set as it is among so many other 17th-century private homes. This one, at Calle Tomás Zerolo 27, houses Artenerife, where you can inspect a wide range of crafts from across the islands. This is one of several outlets around the island for quality handmade products ranging from fine lacework through silk to pottery and traditional musical instruments.

2 Puerto de la Cruz

Puerto de la Cruz, once merely the port for the rich business town of La Orotava high up in the hinterland, transformed itself in the 1960s into Tenerife's principal tourist resort. Although some ugly high-rise hotels mar the skyline, as resorts go it's a mixed and interesting place. Explore the fishing port and what remains of the old centre, lounge about in the shallow sea-water pools of Lago Martiánez or head for the spacious black beach of Playa Jardín.

Beaches

Odd really. First they built the beach resort and then they thought about the beaches. The minuscule strips of volcanic sand and rock that constitute **Playa San Telmo** can hardly be thought of as a beach. So just to the east the Lanzarote artist César Manrique designed the pleasing **Lago Martiánez**, a leisure complex based on sky-blue, sea-water pools.

If you prefer to cavort in the ocean waves, then head west for **Playa Jardín**. This broad strand of fine volcanic sand has been turned into an attractive leisure area. The beach, as long as you don't mind the colour, is as good as any, studded with deep-black, volcanic boulders and palms. In the background is the garden part, an extensive maze of palms and other trees. A restaurant and snack bar complete the offerings.

Look out for intricate detail on the houses – this one is on Calle San Felipe

At the eastern edge of the beach rise the forbidding walls of the **Castillo San Felipe**, an early 17th-century emplacement built to help defend the old port from unwelcome visitors. Classical and folk evening concerts are frequently staged here. Tickets available on site.

Town Centre

Back in the centre of town, you can indulge in a little
sightseeing. At the western end of Lago Martiánez, the tiny
Ermita de San Telmo is a chapel founded in 1780 by the
seamen's guild. Things have changed: this is now the place to
hear Mass in German.

About 200m (220 yards) west, Puerto de la Cruz's main
church, the **Iglesia de Nuestra Señora de la Peña de
Francia** (Church of Our Lady of the Rock of France), a sturdy
baroque structure filled with gaudy *retablos,* presides over
Plaza de la Iglesia.

Around the Port

Closer to the waterfront are two well-preserved traditional
Canary Island mansions. The **Casa de Miranda**, has exquisite
carved teak balconies and interior, and was built in 1730 and
now serves as a restaurant of the same name.

Overlooking the little fishing port on Calle Lonjas is the
Casa de la Aduana, once the Customs house. You can enter
the courtyard to admire the timberwork and enter rooms used
for the sale of island crafts, food and wine.

The **Museo Arqueológico** (Archaeology Museum) is in
fact a small Guanche (➤ 13) ceramics display. The simple
bowls, plates, mugs and even a couple of *amphorae* are the
main clues to how Guanche society worked. Housed in an
exquisitely restored mansion, it warrants a quick visit if
only as a reminder that the islands do not have a solely
Spanish history.

Looking down on the rest of the town is the **Parque
Taoro**. By day you can meander in the sculpture gardens or
kids' aquatic park. The fine mansion at the heart of the park
was, until late 2005, home to the town's **casino** but it stands
neglected with no firm date for redevelopment in place.

Out of Town

About 1.5km (1 mile) from the centre of Puerto de la Cruz
on an inland road leading to the T5 motorway is the 17th-
century **Jardín Botánico** (Botanical Garden). In 1788, King

**Parque
Tajinaste is
a hotel quite
near to the
botanical
gardens**

Charles III of Spain ordered the creation of this garden so that a wide collection of tropical species might be grown on Spanish soil in the appropriate climate. The good king clearly had strong views on matters floral (was it to do with his unusually prominent nose?) for he was behind the creation of the Botanical Gardens in Madrid as well. The garden has some extraordinary specimens, like the huge Moreton Bay fig tree near the entrance and a twisted, tangled Brasilian rubber tree.

The bells toll for all in the baroque belfry of the Iglesia de Nuestra Señora de la Peña de Francia

TAKING A BREAK

Have a drink at any of the outdoor cafés on central **Plaza del Charco**. For a fine meal in cosy surroundings, reserve a table at the 18th-century **Casa de Miranda** on **Calle Santo Domingo**.

🚩 **177 F5**

Casa de la Aduana
✉ Calle Lonjas ☎ 922/378-103
🕐 Mon–Sat 10–8

Parque Taoro
✉ Carretera de Taoro 🕐 All day
💰 Free

Iglesia de Nuestra Señora de la Peña de Francia
✉ Plaza de la Iglesia s/n 🕐 Daily 8–1, 5–8
💰 Free

Jardín Botánico
✉ Calle Retama 2 ☎ 922/383-572 🕐 Apr–Sep daily 9–7, Oct–Mar daily 9–6 💰 Moderate

Lago Martiánez
✉ Avenida de Colón s/n ☎ 922/385-955 🕐 Daily May–Sep 10–7, Oct–Apr 10–6 💰 Moderate

Museo Arqueológico
✉ Calle del Lomo 9/a ☎ 922/371-465, www.arqueopc.museum 🕐 Tue–Sat 10–1, 5–9, Sun 10–1 💰 Moderate

PUERTO DE LA CRUZ: INSIDE INFO

Top tip The little **ceramic figurine in Room 5** of the Museo Arqueológico, one of the only such objects found in Tenerife, is a source of constant curiosity. Does it represent a man or a god? What significance might it have had in the Stone-Age minds of the Guanches? Guesses abound but there is little certainty as to its true meaning.

Hidden gem The **area around the Museo Arqueológico**, with its traditional houses and plethora of restaurants, has a homey flavour altogether lacking around Lago Martiánez, which has more of the classic resort feel about it.

3 Icod de los Vinos

A wine-belt town high up above the rugged northwest coast of Tenerife, Icod de los Vinos has for years made a good part of its living from a single tree. The bizarre shape of the *drago*, the huge dragon tree, claimed to be more than 1,000 years old, keeps visitors pouring in. The grand old plant is worth the effort but there is more to Icod, including a fascinating butterfly museum and a pleasing, compact old centre.

If you drive into town, signs to the **Parque del Drago** will lead you to a parking area where you can leave the car and buy a ticket that includes entry into the gardens where the dragon tree stands. The price also covers the option of a little yellow train to take you to the park. If you just want to contemplate the tree from a (short) distance in Plaza de la Iglesia, park elsewhere.

The gnarled and sinewy **dragon tree** is 15m (99-feet) tall and 6m (20 feet) in diameter at its base. In the 1,000–2,000 years that this old specimen has been around (dragon trees don't have rings so estimating their age is a rough science), it has put out an extraordinarily complex web of branches. The tree's sap is known as "dragon's blood" as it turns red on contact with the air. The "blood" traditionally was used for medicinal purposes and as a natural dye.

The ancient drago (dragon tree) of Icod de los Vinos has become a symbol of Tenerife over the centuries

Around the tree spreads a modest **botanical garden**, including several rather young dragon trees that pale into insignificance next to the old boy.

Virtually next door to the Parque del Drago is a lepidopterist's dream, the **Mariposario del Drago** (Butterfly Museum), where hundreds of exotic butterflies flit about in a tropical garden. Some have been bred here, others are imported. These pretty creatures live only for about three weeks on average. The 70-minute documentary gets up close to the insect world.

Equal measures of patience would have been required by one Jerónimo de Espellosa y Villabriga, a Spaniard living in Cuba who, in 1668, completed, after five years, the remarkable silver cross in the **Museo de la Iglesia de San Marcos**. The museum is little more than a room in the church of the same name, and the cross is the only item of serious interest. At 2.45m (8 feet) high and weighing 48.3kg (106 pounds), it is a marvel of detailed work, looking more like a complex piece of embroidery than a heavy chunk of precious metal.

This *Danaus plexippus* butterfly was spotted at the Icod butterfly museum

TAKING A BREAK

Stop for a coffee in the snack bar at the **Parque del Drago**. Otherwise head to the bar in the bandstand in shady **Plaza de Cáceres**, which is linked to Plaza de la Iglesia.

✚ 177 D4

Parque del Drago
✉ Plaza de la Consitucion ☎ 922/814-510
🕐 Daily 10–6 💵 Moderate

Mariposario del Drago
✉ Avenida de Canarias s/n
☎ 922/815-167;
www.mariposario.com 🕐 Daily 9–6 (an hour longer in summer) 💵 Expensive

Museo de la Iglesia de San Marcos
✉ Plaza de la Iglesia ☎ 922/810-695
🕐 Mon–Sat 9–1:30, 4–6:30 💵 Inexpensive

ICOD DE LOS VINOS: INSIDE INFO

Top tip About 200m (220 yards) along Calle San Antonio from Plaza de la Constitución, in the little square called Plazuela Cabrera Mejías, is another, **smaller dragon tree** known affectionately as the Drago Chico ("little dragon").

Hidden gem If you have a little extra time, head for **Plaza de la Constitución**, a quick walk north of the Parque del Drago and part of the compact old town. Among its mansions is the **Casa-Museo "Los Cáceres"** (Plaza de la Constitución 1, daily 10–1, 5–8, free), a sturdy neoclassical house built early in the 19th century. Inside is a beautiful *patio* dominated by grand timber columns and an enclosed gallery. A permanent gallery features works by artist Guillermo Sureda and the *casa* hosts temporary art and photography exhibitions.

4 Garachico

Not to be beaten by the molten lava that flowed into, and destroyed much of, the busy port town of Garachico in 1706, its people met the challenge and rebuilt their town, which today is one of the most charming urban legacies on Tenerife.

The small bay just west of the centre was once its main port, although nothing remains to remind us of Garachico's commercial heyday. In front of the town's esplanade are a couple of rocky inlets known as **El Caletón**, formed by the cooling lava flows of 1706 and now used as natural pools.

The compact old town of Garachico, rebuilt in the 18th century, is an inviting place

Castles and Convents

Standing silent watch over the inlets is the brooding **Castillo de San Miguel**, a typical defensive fort, built of the dark local volcanic rock. Inside is a collection of sea shells, fossils, stuffed sea creatures (including a tortoise and a sea horse), one *live* tortoise and a series of fossils and minerals.

The greatest attraction is the former **Convento de San Francisco**, now home to the Casa de la Cultura (House of Culture). When you walk in to the former convent you are greeted by two beautiful courtyards. The first is simple with slender timber columns supporting the first-floor balconies. The second, which served as the main cloister, is enriched by palm trees and rose bushes. The ground floor has an odd collection whose most intriguing element is the old black-and-white photos of Garachico. The adjacent **church**, Iglesia de Nuestra Señora de los Ángeles, if open, is worth a look for the exquisite *mudéjar* ceiling. The church is a curiously lopsided affair, its nave flanked on one side by a aisle of equal width in which you'll see the town's *pasos* (Easter procession floats) stored. The **Iglesia de Santa Ana**, dominating the adjacent **Plaza de Arriba**, was largely rebuilt and equipped with a six-storey bell tower in the early 18th century after lava and fire finished off most of its 16th-century predecessor.

The Castillo de San Miguel, overlooking the sea, houses an eclectic collection

Mansions and Museums

On the same square is a noble mansion, the **Casa Palacio de los Condes de la Gomera**, on whose ground floor temporary exhibitions of local art and photography are occasionally organised. The handful of lanes around here and the pleasant **Plaza de Juan González de la Torre** all make for a rewarding stroll.

If you head east of the old centre you will find the beautifully shaded **Plaza de Santo Domingo** and the 17th-century **Convento de Santo Domingo**. With its timber balconies and stonework, it houses the hospital and a now-closed art museum. Finally, towards the western exit of the town, in front of the big farming co-operative, is the **Museo de la Carpintería Antigua**. You can admire a limited display of traditional wood-working instruments and some intriguing items made with them. The museum really serves as a bit of a front for the business of selling local wines, banana liqueur and other souvenirs.

TAKING A BREAK

Try **Isla Baja** near the Castillo de San Miguel for snacks or traditional fish dishes.

✚ 176 C4

Tourist Information Office
✉ Calle Estéban de Ponte 5 ☎ 922/133-461 🕐 Mon–Sat 11–3

Castillo de San Miguel
✉ Tomé Cano s/n 🕐 Daily 10–1, 3–6 💷 Inexpensive

Convento de San Francisco
✉ Plazoleta de la Libertad s/n 🕐 Mon–Fri 10–7, Sat–Sun 10–3
💷 Inexpensive

Museo de la Carpintería Antigua
✉ Avenida República de Venezuela 17 ☎ 922/ 830-333 🕐 Daily 9–7
💷 Free

GARACHICO: INSIDE INFO

Top tip Remember to take your swimwear to Garachico. If the sun's out there's nothing more refreshing than a dip in the lava rockpools that front the town in a permanent reminder of the 1706 volcanic eruption.

Hidden gem Don't leave town without at least having had a look inside the wonderful **Hotel La Quinta Roja** (Glorieta de San Francisco s/n, tel: 922/133-377, www.quintaroja.com) opposite the former Convento de San Francisco. This deep orange mansion, impressively restored and well worth splurging on as an overnight stay, has two adjoining *patios* so inviting you will find it hard to resist taking a seat. And then there's the sauna...

5 Masca

The dramatic location high in the Teno Massif makes the hamlet of Masca one of Tenerife's most engaging stops. Take one of the walks, including a challenging hike down to the coast. It's also a lovely place to watch a splendid sunset.

A Long and Winding Road

Whichever way you approach, from the north or the south, arriving in Masca (600m/1,968 feet) is a theatrical process. From the north you follow a meandering road through farmland and rougher territory, including a couple of extraordinary lookout points, before dipping down gently for the final approach. This takes you through an initial huddle of half a dozen houses and immediately after, on the left, a gushing cascade. From the south, the introduction is altogether more sudden. After passing through humdrum Santiago del Teide and a quick ascent, you drop into a series

Masca is little more than a scattering of houses perched prettily at the head of a steep valley

Hiking through the spectacular Masca gorge

of dizzying bends to reach the town. All the while you are presented with long views along the **Barranco de Masca**, the gorge in which the hamlet rises, and out to sea. A *terraza* is on this road shortly before arrival in Masca and is perfectly placed for watching the sun as it sets.

Fire

On the night of 31st July 2007, 18,000ha (45,000 acres) of forest on the hillsides of northwestern Tenerife succumbed to a devastating forest fire, and the village of Masca and the Barranco where caught at the epicentre. Though no-one in the village was killed, half the buildings were destroyed. The villagers vowed to rebuild and many are in the process of restarting their lives and livelihoods. Masca is rising like a phoenix from the ashes, the new buildings retaining the style of those consumed by the flames. Nature is also playing its part, blanketing the hillsides with swathes of fresh green. However, parts of the Barranco may be off-limits to the public and you should obey any signs you see – these are in place to allow the vegetation to recover.

Walking the Barranco

If you want to walk down into the gorge, follow the central path past the houses and you'll see how it quickly reverts to a dirt trail. The hike there and back will take six to seven hours. Alternatively, you can arrange to meet a tour boat at 3pm to take you to Los Gigantes (► 102), saving you the uphill trek.

TAKING A BREAK

Chez Arlette (► 110) by the church has excellent views and home-made traditional dishes.

➕ 176 B3

MASCA: INSIDE INFO

Top tip If you are here in the **first week of December**, enquire about Masca's **Fiesta de la Consolación**. This is a religious feast day when villagers dress in traditional clothes and musicians break out their *timples* (like a ukelele) to liven up the atmosphere after the solemn religious procession.

6 Acantilado de los Gigantes

Uncompromising walls of volcanic rock that drop sheer into the ocean mark the southern end of the Teno Massif's rugged coast. Known as the Acantilado de los Gigantes (Giants' Cliff), they are a formidable piece of natural architecture. Directly to the south is a beach, La Canalita, and this, together with the promise of year-round sunshine, set off a tourist boom. Two interlocking resorts, Los Gigantes and Puerto de Santiago, spread south in a blaze of brilliant white apartments and hotels, restaurants and bars.

Giants' Cliff

Although you can relax on the beach and observe the staggering 500–600m (1,640–1,968 foot) cliffs, a better option is to take one of the many **boat excursions** that go up close and allow you some swimming time in their shadow. There are several variations on these tours. They generally combine the cliffs with some whale- and dolphin-spotting or a trip up the coast to the little beach at the bottom of the Barranco de Masca gorge (▶ 101). If you are interested in walking down, but not up, the gorge, you can arrange for one of these tour boats to pick you up on the beach after trekking down from Masca and to take you back to Los Gigantes. Enquire about the *Nashira Uno* boat (tel: 922/861-918) which operates from the yacht harbour in Los Gigantes. Travel agents throughout the two resorts can help.

Volcanic cliffs provide a backdrop to the harbour at Los Gigantes

The cliffs near Los Gigantes stretch into the distance

In large part due to the cliffs, **Los Gigantes** is more appealing than Puerto de Santiago, which spreads several kilometres along the coast below Los Gigantes (the two resorts are supposedly separated by 1km (0.5 miles) but you'd be hard pressed to identify the dividing line).

In the 1980s **Puerto de Santiago**, with its nearby pleasant black-sand beach, **Playa de la Arena**, was still a largely tourist-free fishing settlement. What has replaced it is fairly tranquil but no sense of the original village remains. Instead the usual chorus line of British and Irish pubs, full English breakfasts and endless tourist souvenirs have settled here.

The water off this stretch of coast is considered some of the clearest for **diving** and there is no shortage of dive shops that hire out gear, organise dive trips and run courses (usually PADI) for beginners and more advanced divers.

TAKING A BREAK

Restaurante Pancho (➤ 110) on Playa de la Arena has a spacious setting and Canarian menu.

➕ 176 B3

ACANTILADO DE LOS GIGANTES: INSIDE INFO

Hidden gem To get an idea of what Puerto de Santiago might once have been like, head south along the coast road to **Playa de San Juan**, a village with a small grey beach that still lives largely from fishing. A couple of side roads and paths along the next 10km (6 miles) south also reveal a handful of secluded coves and rocky points.

At Your Leisure

7 Loro Parque

This ever-popular private zoo keeps adding new attractions, the latest a children's section called Kinderlandia. It all started with parrots and the flock of them here is claimed to be the biggest in the world. They are just one of the attractions in this hybrid setting, where alligators, gorillas, monkeys, chimpanzees, jaguars, tigers, giant turtles, pelicans, flamingos and other animals live side by side. You can attend dolphin and sea-lion shows, watch parrots (*loros*) ride bicycles, or admire the sharks.

The park also has a wealth of tropical plants. Join the **Behind the Scenes tour**, during which you will see where the dolphins train, where the gorillas sleep and where new fish and sea horses are kept in quarantine. A free **mini-train** picks up visitors from Avenida Venezuela, close to Lago Martiánez in Puerto de la Cruz, every 20 minutes.

Loro Parque also has the distinction of having the world's largest collection of porcelain parrots, many produced in the 18th century in the famous porcelain factory at Meissen in Germany. The Loro Parque Foundation, the charitable arm of Loro Parque, funds worldwide projects related to parrot protection and population preservation.

➕ 177 F5 ✉ 1.5km (1 mile) west of Puerto de la Cruz ☎ 922/373-841; www.loroparque. com ◷ Daily 8:30–6:45 💰 Expensive

8 Bananera El Guanche

A visit here, if somewhat touristy, is instructive on the history of bananas on the island. It is also an impressive garden, filled with weird and wonderful trees and plants from all over the world. When you enter you will be ushered off to watch a brief but informative video (in a range of languages) on just what a banana is. The plantation's owners claim that eating a banana is as good for you as eating a steak, but non-fattening.

Equipped with this knowledge, you can proceed into the gardens,

Large crowds turn out for the daily orca performances at Loro Parque

where bananas give way to all sorts of other things, among them papayas, Australian macadamia nuts, avocados, pineapples, mangoes, Kenyan coffee trees, cotton, Mexican yucca and *chirimoyas* (or *cherimoya*), a tropical fruit.

You can also see the striking *strelitzia* or bird of paradise flowers that have become an island emblem and buy local honey and palm syrup (*miel de palma*).

For those without cars, a regular free bus (look out for the yellow Bananera El Guanche sign) shuttles from central Puerto de la Cruz.

➕ 180 A3 ✉ 2km (1 mile) out of Puerto de la Cruz on the road linking the city with the T5 motorway ☎ 922/331-853; www.bananeraelguanche.com ⏱ Daily 9–6 💷 Expensive

9 Pueblo Chico

Pueblo Chico is just that: a "little village". Indeed this is a trip into the Canary Islands in miniature, with scale models of everything from the town of La Laguna to a Guanche village scene. A good one for the kids, it is just off trhe TF5 motorway between La Orotava and Puerto de la Cruz.

➕ 177 F5 ✉ Camino Cruz de los Martillos 62 ☎ 922/334-060; www.pueblochico.com ⏱ Daily May–Sep 9–7, Oct–Apr 9–6 💷 Expensive

Set deep in a protected bay, Playa de San Marcos is the perfect getaway from Icod

10 San Juan de la Rambla

San Juan seems a quiet village. At its tiny historic core, made up of Plaza de San Juan and adjoining Plaza Rosario Oramas, are a pleasing little church and typically 18th-century Canarian mansions. The old town sits on a ledge just north of the TF5 highway and then slips down to the rugged coast. A newer area stands further up the hill.

➕ 177 E5 ✉ 11km (7 miles) west of Puerto de la Cruz

11 Playa de San Marcos

A black-sand crescent beach set deep in a protected bay and surrounded by forbidding rock walls rising abruptly away from the shore, the Playa de San Marcos is just 2.5km (1.5 miles) north of Icod de los Vinos (➤ 96). The parking areas that snake uphill back from the beach are indication enough of its popularity. The beach is backed by a handful of restaurants, with balconies overlooking the sand.

➕ 176 C4 ✉ 2.5km (1.5 miles) north of Icod de los Vinos

12 Arguayo

Seemingly left to its own devices on a side road running parallel to the north–south TF820 highway, Arguayo

is a detour for those with time on their hands in the Puerto de Santiago area. At the steep northern end of the village is the **Centro Alfarero Cha Domitila**, a small ceramics museum and workshop. The tumbledown house with its uneven *patio* has been a ceramics workshop since the mid-1980s. You can see all sorts of simple traditional bowls and other objects, watch them being made and, of course, buy some.

➕ 176 B3 ✉ Centro Alfarero Cha Domitila, Carretera General 37 ☎ 922/863-465
🕐 Tue–Sat 10–1, 4–7, Sun 10–2 💲 Free

🔟 Buenavista del Norte

Living in one of the island's most remote communities, the people of Buenavista del Norte are renowned for their self-sufficiency and still make a living from the land. Founded in 1498 amid magnificent mountainscapes, there's an intriguing mix of Guancha, Portuguese and Spanish blood in the ancestry of today's townspeople, indeed Portuguese script appears in the original city archives dated 1512. The historic town centres on the 16th-century **Iglesia de Los Remedios** while traditional stone farmhouses (many now abandoned) dot the surrounding hills. Don't forget to make a stop at **Pasteleria El Aderno** on Calle La Alhóndiga

The Punta de Teno, with its abrupt coastline, is one of Tenerife's wildest locations

(➤ 111) to buy some of the island's best cakes and pastries.
➕ 176 B4 ✉ 75km (46 miles) west of Santa Cruz de Tenerife

🔟 Punta de Teno

Punta de Teno is one of the oldest existing volcanic outflows on the island. Millions of years ago what the Guanches thought off as a devil coughed up its molten anger in this direction. Now stark, rocky cliffs fold back in on themselves towards the south from this westernmost tip of Tenerife. The scenery has an untamed, wild feel unmatched elsewhere on the island. From in front of the Punta de Teno lighthouse you can make out the coastline of La Palma and La Gomera on a clear day.

Walkers can make a long half-day of it by following the signs to hike inland and up to the heights of the Teno Massif.

It is best to do this walk equipped with good hiking maps, which are available at tourist offices, and to allow about four hours for the trip there and back.
➕ 176 A4 ✉ 18km (11 miles) west of Garachico

Where to...
Stay

Prices

The following price ranges are for a double room in high season, IGIC sales tax included. Rates vary seasonally.

€ under €70   €€ €70–120   €€€ over €120

LA OROTAVA

Hotel Alhambra €€

A magical Moorish fantasy has been carved out of an 18th-century villa on the edge of the old town. Much of the styling is dominated by dazzling white horseshoe arches. Bathroom tiling is reminiscent of Morocco. Five spacious doubles and two suites are on offer, and extras include a garden, pool, gym, sauna and glass ceiling patio.

✚ 180 A3 ☒ Calle Nicandro Gonzáles Borges 19 ☎ 922/320-434; www.alhambra-teneriffa.com

Victoria €€

This 17th-century mansion has been thoughtfully restored in a style befitting its age and dignity. The glass-roofed restaurant is one of its most attractive features with waitresses dressed in traditional Canarian costumes. The rooms are decently furnished, and the rooftop terrace has lovely views towards the distant sea. During the Corpus Cristi festivities in June (▶ 10), La Orotava is besieged with visitors and advance booking is advisable.

✚ 180 A3 ☒ Calle H Apolinar 8 ☎ 922/331-683; www.hotelruralvictoria.com

PUERTO DE LA CRUZ

Botánico €€€

Just across the road from the Jardín Botánico (▶ 94), this hotel displays a green-fingered touch in its grounds – a lush and shady sanctuary of fountains, fish-pools and billowing vegetation. The interior is just as well kept, with classic furnishings and spacious public areas. A host of luxurious accoutrements keeps its well-heeled clientele happy, from sports facilities to spa and beauty salons, and three highly regarded restaurants. A pianist plays in the cocktail lounge, and shuttle buses minimise the 2km (1.2-mile) journey to the centre of Puerto. Rooms are predictably elegant and comfortable.

✚ 177 F5 ☒ Avenida Richard J Yeoward 1, Urb. El Botánico ☎ 922/381-400; www.hotelbotanico.com

Marquesa €€

Right in the pedestrianised heart of Puerto's old town, this beautifully restored 18th-century Canarian building faces the church square. Restaurant terrace tables by the main entrance give a grandstand seat for watching the street entertainers and mime artists who throng the resort during the height of the tourist season. Inside there's an airy courtyard foyer, which is a nice getaway spot from the crowds outside. A maze of bright, simple rooms occupies the modern extensions at the rear. There's a tiny splash-pool on the roof terrace with a great view of Mount Teide.

✚ 177 F5 ☒ Calle Quintana 11 ☎ 922/383-151; www.hotelmarquesa.com

Monopol €€

The Monopol is decorated in traditional Canarian style with ornate wooden balconies and a delightful jungle-like atrium where huge cheese-plants scramble towards the ceiling and wicker sofas. Owned by the same family for generations, the staff are friendly, and personal touches, like the flower petals strewn daily on the entrance steps, add to its charm. Rooms vary in size, shape and style, but are cheerfully decorated and have neat, modern bathrooms. A small pool and jacuzzi on a rear sun terrace offer hot and cold dips.

⊞ 177 F5 ⊠ Calle Quintana 15 ☎ 922/384-611; www.hotelmonopoltenerife.com

Hotel Tigaiga €€

Although it wouldn't win any prizes for its late 1950s boxy design, the family-owned Tigaiga gets great reviews for its service and value for money. A robust eco-management policy has resulted in a number of awards from internationally recognised bodies, including the European Union EMAS scheme. Lush palms and 5000sq m (50,000sq ft) of tropical gardens (the founder was an amateur botanist) soften the exterior and there's a good sized free-form pool on hand for the 76 rooms. There are lovely sea views from around

the grounds. Rooms have a bright cheery feel, and each has a balcony.
⊞ 177 F5 ⊠ Parque Taora 28 ☎ 922/383-500; www.tigaiga.com

GARACHICO

Caserío Los Partidos €€

This charming little place is in Tenerife's hilly northwest corner, with views of Mount Teide. Each of the rooms has an open fireplace and immaculate bathroom. Terraces and courtyards bright with flowers and fountains spill around the building. This isolated retreat is a long way from the congested coastal resorts, and it appeals primarily to walkers and visitors who value peace and quiet. A car is essential if you plan to do any exploring.
⊞ 176 C4 ⊠ Los Partidos, San Jose de los Llanos, El Tanque ☎ 922/693-090; www.caserio-lospartidos.com

San Roque €€€

This imaginative little hotel is a lovingly restored 17th-century

house with an aristocratic pedigree. Modern sculpture and statuary grace the inner courtyard while sleek sofas and Bauhaus chairs invite casual indolence, along with a photogenic mosaic swimming pool. The rooms revel in cool furnishings and state-of-the-art bathrooms and there's good food prepared by its resident owners.
⊞ 176 C4 ⊠ Calle Esteban de Ponte 32 ☎ 922/133-435; www.hotelsanroque.com

ACANTILADO DE LOS GIGANTES

Hotel Costa Los Gigantes Suites & Spa Resort €€€

The paint was just dry on this lovely new hotel in the summer of 2008 and it's been designed with modern family holiday-makers in mind. This is an all-suites property that operates on full-board. There's a great range of activities on site from a kids' club and free WiFi in reception, to an enormous pool and a full-service spa, so it's the perfect place for recharging the

batteries. The 481 suites share seven restaurants – with four à la carte options. A dress code applies in the evenings – men must wear full shoes and long trousers.
⊞ 176 B3 ⊠ Calle Juan Manuel Capdevielle 8, Playa de la Arena ☎ 922/862-772; www.springhoteles.com

El Sombrero Apartments €

The crisp, clean, but basic three-storey apartments at El Sombrero are set around a small pool. This is a no-frills property but impeccably kept and popular with families who want to do their own thing. The units are simply furnished with traditional Canarian furniture mixed with chintzy touches. Each has a good sized balcony. Some have views across the resort down to the sea, around a 15-minute walk away. The apartments are situated at the top of Los Gigantes, so if you're not fit you'll certainly need a taxi back from the beach.
⊞ 176 B3 ⊠ Avenida Marítima 28 ☎ 922/861-353; www.el-sombrero.com

Where to...
Eat and Drink

Prices

The following price ranges indicate what you can expect to pay per person for a meal, including drinks, tax and tip.

€ under €20 €€ €20–40 €€€ over €40

LA OROTAVA

Casa Lercaro €–€€

This is another rambling mansion reborn as a restaurant and shop for island artisan products. Much of the pleasure of eating here is the 17th-century setting. You can dine in one of several indoor and outdoor courtyard enclaves. Food is hearty and comforting Spanish fare. After eating wander around the house and its gardens.

🚹 180 A3 ☒ Calle Colegio 7 ☎ 922/326-204, www.casalercaro.com ☻ Daily noon–4:30, 7–10

Restaurant Lucas Maes €€€

One of a new breed of fusion restaurants, this one is presided over by its dynamic young chef Lucas Maes. Housed in a historic mansion the dining room has received a contemporary make-over and there's a terrace for al fresco lunches and dinners. The menu oozes luxury dishes such as lobster with truffle oil, but everything is served with a light touch and a play of flavours and textures.

🚹 180 A3 ☒ Calle Barranco de Arena 53 ☎ 922/321-159 ☻ Tue–Sat 1–3:30, 7–11. Closed Sun and Mon

Sabor Canario €€

The former Museo del Pueblo Guanche in the historic heart of La Orotava is a showcase for Canarian crafts and food products in a building dating from 1595. Attached to it is a lovely restaurant serving local dishes – try conejo en salmorejo (braised rabbit) or ropa vieja (literally "old clothes", a classic Canarian stew). The patio tables in its plant-filled courtyard are enticing.

🚹 180 A3 ☒ Calle Carrera 17 ☎ 922/323-793; www.saborcanario.com ☻ Mon–Sat noon–4:30, 7:30–10

PUERTO DE LA CRUZ

La Gañania €€€

This traditional Canarian house Pedro Gonzalez Rodriguez Dios is a life-force. This young Spanish chef has been rising through the ranks and had accolades from the press in Madrid, especially for his mouth-watering desserts. He concentrates on Canarian influences and shops in the markets on the island for ultra-fresh seasonal produce. Even the bread is made on site – so you know you are eating true restaurant cuisine. The hilltop setting in a pretty rustic dining room is delightful.

🚹 177 F5 ☒ Camino Durazno 71 ☎ 922/371-000 ☻ Wed–Sun 1–4, 7–11. Closed Mon and Tue

La Magnolia €€€

One of Puerto de la Cruz's top restaurants in the La Paz district, offering superb Catalan and international cooking in an elegant, modern setting. The speciality is fish; enormous portions appear from an open kitchen, often dressed in pungent garlic sauces. Be sure to reserve a table in advance.

🚹 177 F5 ☒ Avenida Marqués de Villanueva del Prado s/n ☎ 922/385-614 ☻ Wed–Mon 1–4, 7–midnight

Mesón El Monasterio €€

High in the hills behind Puerto, this unusual restaurant has been skilfully converted from a rambling 17th-century convent. Farm animals and poultry wander freely around the grounds. A maze of rustic dining rooms and terrace tables provide space for Canarian roast and chargrilled specials and a huge range of wines. The staff are friendly and helpful.

➕ 177 E4 ☒ La Montañeta, Los Realejos ☎ 922/340-707 ⏱ Daily 10am–11pm

ACANTILADO DE LOS GIGANTES

Restaurante Pancho €€

One of the island's best chefs has built up the reputation of this place over several years. On its spacious terrace tables shaded by lush foliage overlook Playa de la Arena's lovely beach. An imaginative Canarian menu features rice and fish dishes; but snacks, drinks and delicious cakes are available all afternoon too.

➕ 176 B3 ☒ Playa de la Arena, Puerto de Santiago ☎ 922/861-323 ⏱ Tue–Sun 1–4, 7–11; closed Jun

GARACHICO

Restaurante La Perla €

Garachico is a simple place and the same can be said of its cooking, but at La Perla you'll get lashings of the stuff. Tables sport red-and-white gingham and the menu is evenly divided between fish and meat.

➕ 176 C4 ☒ Calle de 18 Julio ☎ 922/830-286 ⏱ Tue–Sun 1–4, 7–10:30

MASCA

Chez Arlette €

The attractive location with spectacular valley views makes this simple place one of the most popular in Masca. Despite numbers of visitors, the rustic style persists on its shaded terrace decked with wooden furnishings and a mass of plant life. The menu is varied and inexpensive and you can wash everything down with home-made lemonade or local wine.

➕ 176 B3 ☒ La Piedra, Masca ☎ 922/863-459 ⏱ Sun–Thu 11–7

Where to...
Shop

Puerto de la Cruz is the main shopping centre in this region. Shopping hours are long; many outlets stay open until quite late in the evening. Inland, La Orotava offers some of the best of the island's crafts.

CRAFTS

Distinctive Canarian *bordados* (hand embroidery), *calados* (drawn threadwork) and lace can be found in many shops. In Puerto de la Cruz and La Orotava, some craft shops are tourist attractions in their own right because of their settings in restored old timbered houses. Some have museums or restaurants on site. The best-known is the **Casa de los Balcones** (branches at Calle San Francisco 3, La Orotava or Paseo de San Telmo, Puerto de la Cruz). Also worth seeing for their architecture as well as their wares are **Casa del Turista** (Calle San Francisco 4, La Orotava), **Casa Torrehermosa** (Calle Tomás Zerolo, La Orotava), **Pueblo Guanche** (Calle Carrera 7, La Orotava) and **Casa Iriarte** (Calle San Juan 17, Puerto de la Cruz).

Arguayo is known for its **pottery**, shaped by hand to Guanche designs without a potter's wheel. The rugged results are on display at the **Centro Alfarero** (Tue–Sat 10–1, 4–7, Sun 10–2), easily spotted on the main road through the village.

Traditional **ceramics** are also sold at the studio workshop in the 17th-century **Museo de Cerámica** (Casa Tafuriaste, Calle León 3, La Orotava, tel: 922/321-447; Mon–Fri 10–6, Sat 10–2).

Where to...
Be Entertained

NIGHTLIFE

In **Puerto de la Cruz** in the early evening the seafront and the old town plazas buzz in a classic Latin *paseo*. Night owls should head for the streets behind the **Lido** (Avenida del Generalísimo/Calle Hoya), where clubs **Joy** (Calle Obispo Pérez Cáceres), **El Teatro Lounge Bar** (Calle Puerto Viejo) and **Acuzar** (Calle Iriarte) are the cool spots.

Los Gigantes is mostly quiet at night apart from a few music bars like **Highland Paddy's** (Avenida Marítima, Playa de la Arena).

CASINO AND CABARET

Puerto de la Cruz Casino sits in the heart of Lido Martiánez

(Avenida de Colón, tel: 922/380-550) surrounded by the stunning pools. It offers American roulette, black jack and one-armed bandits. Take photo ID to gain entry.

Andromeda at the Isla del Lago (tel: 922/383-852) and **Oasis Orotava Palace** (tel: 922/382-960) puts on glitzy cabaret venues with dinner shows and international artistes. The **Sol Puerto de la Cruz** hotel (tel: 922/384-011) has live music every night.

DAYTIME DIVERSIONS

Abaco (Urb El Durazno, Calle Casa Grande, tel: 922/374-811, www. abacotenerife.com; daily 10:30–1:30, 8pm–2:30am) is a well-restored 18th-century Canarian house that was originally the governor's mansion.

Summer **craft fairs** (*ferias de artesanía*) are held between May and October in many older towns, including Los Realejos, La Orotava, Santiago del Teide, El Tanque, Buenavista del Norte, Garachico and San Juan de la Rambla.

HOME-GROWN PRODUCE

Northwest Tenerife is one of the most fertile parts of the island. An old **banana** farm near Puerto de la Cruz, **Bananera El Guanche** has diversified into a worthwhile tourist attraction (▶ 104).

Icod de los Vinos is renowned as a **wine-producing** area. Visitors to the ancient **Parque del Drago** (▶ 96) will almost certainly be invited to taste (and preferably buy) some locally made *malvasía* (malmsey) in the *bodegas* and souvenir shops.

The **Bar Restaurant Chinyero** (Avenida General Franco 2B, Valle Santiago, tel: 922/864-040; www.barrest-chinyero.com) at

Santiago del Teide serves good Canarian wines with *tapas*.

Garachico's **Centro de Artesanía el Limonero** (Avenida Tomé Cano s/n) has a variety of wine and cheese for sale. At Buenavista del Norte, **Pastelería El Aderno** (Calle La Alhóndiga, 8, tel: 922/127-368; www.eladerno. com) is a prize-winning cake shop making traditional island specialities.

MARKETS

Puerto de la Cruz's daily produce market is held in a modern building on Avenida de Blas Pérez González, while souvenir sellers set out their wares to attract tourists along the seafront and in the old town.

Every Monday, African traders congregate on the main road at Alcalá with the usual souvenirs. Farmer's markets are held at **Playa de San Juan** (Wed morning) and **Garachico** (first Sun of each month), selling wines, cheese, tomatoes and bananas.

Here you'll see daytime **folklore displays** and shows (10am–1:30pm). The house is transformed into a cocktail lounge and live music venue in the evenings (Mon–Fri 9pm–2:30am, Sat 3:30pm–3am, Sun 3:30pm–2:30am). Puerto's best family day out, however, is a visit to **Loro Parque** (▶ 104). Children of all ages will also enjoy the **Mariposario del Drago** in Icod de los Vinos (▶ 97), a tropical butterfly garden.

GARDENS

The upside of northern Tenerife's damp, cloudy climate is its local vegetation. Puerto de la Cruz's famous **Jardín Botánico** (▶ 94) is essential viewing for anyone keen on plants. Less well-known garden attractions in Puerto de la Cruz include the **Sitio Litre** (La Paz, tel: 922/382-417; daily 9:30–2:30, moderate), a fine orchid collection in an 18th-century colonial mansion, and

the charming **Risco Bello Aquatic Gardens** (Parque Taoro, daily 10–6:30; moderate).

ON THE WATERFRONT

Swimming

Two of the best beaches are Puerto de la Cruz's **Playa Jardín** (▶ 93), and **Playa de la Arena** (▶ 103), near Los Gigantes. Both are artificial, but well kept and attractively landscaped with palms and gardens. **Lago Martiánez** in Puerto de la Cruz (▶ 93) is a splendid lido. You can also swim safely in calm weather in the low-tide lava rockpools of **Garachico**.

Watersports

The clear waters beneath the Acantilado de los Gigantes provide one of the best locations for watersports. **Sailing**, **scuba-diving** and **sport fishing** are especially popular. For information, go to the tourist office in Playa de la Arena (Avenida Marítima 36–37, tel:

922/860-348; Mon–Fri 9:30–3:30, Sat 9:30–12:30) or the Los Gigantes marina (Puerto Deportivo, tel: 922/868-002). For diving courses try the Diving Centre at Los Gigantes marina (tel: 922/860-431; www.divingtenerife. co.uk); in Puerto de la Cruz try Atlantik at Hotel Marítim (tel: 922/362-801).

Boat Trips

Dolphin- and whale-watching are key activities along the west coast. Licensed operators follow strict guidelines. Try the launch **Nashira Uno** (Los Gigantes marina, tel: 922/861-918). Even if you don't spot dolphins or whales, sailing under the Acantilado de los Gigantes is an amazing experience. One or two unusual boats go from here – **Flipper Uno** is a replica of an 18th-century galleon.

MOUNTAIN HIKES

The volcanic Teno Massif is a great place for tough walks with splendid

views. The mountain-gorge village of **Masca** (▶ 100–101), perched on vertiginous, ancient rocks, is a popular starting point. The upper slopes of the **Orotava Valley** offer other excellent walks; the most interesting trails lead around La Caldera and the strange columnar basalt formations of Los Órganos. Numerous guided hikes are available. For more details on routes and guided walks, and for up-to-date information about the effects of the 2007 forest fires, check the information centres at El Palmar or La Caldera.

Gregorio is an escorted walks operator, offering a large number of scenic routes for walkers of all ages and fitness levels (Hotel Tigaiga, Parque Taoro 28, Puerto de la Cruz, tel: 922/383-500; www.gregorio-teneriffa.de).

Another well-known trekking specialist worth contacting is **Gaiatours** (Calle San Agustín 66, Los Realejos, tel: 922/355-272; www.gaiatours.es).

The South

Getting Your Bearings

After the subtropical lushness of the island's north, the centre and south can come as a shock. Indeed, the geological and climatic contrast contributes to Tenerife's fascination. Short drives separate the dizzy heights of Mount Teide from the shimmering sunshine fun of the southern resorts and the drizzly greenery of the north.

Here you'll find the tallest mountain in Spain, the majestic volcanic temple of Mount Teide (3,718m/12,195 feet). Surrounding it are other impressive peaks and a weird landscape. The rain-starved south coast, from the Costa Adeje to Santa Cruz, is remarkably barren. Until the 1960s few people lived in what was considered the unfortunate side of this otherwise blessed isle.

Not so today. As northern Europeans discovered the joys of Atlantic bathing in the year-round sun, the spread of resort development began, wholly engulfing the small fishing villages, like Los Cristianos, that once dozed in mostly penniless isolation. Now Playa de las Américas and the adjoining beaches form an uninterrupted pleasure dome, full of apartments, bars, English breakfasts, watersports and other diversions.

Many come for a week of this alone, which seems a shame. But a couple of days of sun and fun can make a nice counterweight to the exploration of Tenerife's cultural and natural wonders further north.

2313m
Los Mallorquines

El Portillo

Las Cañadas
del Teide

TF-21

3718m   2748m
El Teide   Blanca

**Parque Nacional
del Teide**

1

2712m
Guajara

Cañadas

TF-21

Arico 11

Villa de Arico

El Río

Vilaflor 6

**Granadilla
de Abona 7**

Las Cancelas
Armeñime

Adeje

La Caleta

Arona

San Miguel
de Abona

Torviscas

Costa Adeje 2   **Siam
Park 5**

Valle de
San Lorenzo

Chuchurumbache

TF-1

**Playa de las
Américas 2**

Los Cristianos 2

Guaza

Reina Sofía

El Médano 9

Palm-Mar

Los Abrigos

Punta de la Rasca

**Las
Galletas 8 8**

**Costa del
Silencio**

Punta
Salema

Page 113: The views from Las Rocas stretch towards La Gomera

★ Don't Miss

At Your Leisure

Las Caletillas

4 Candelaria

Arafo

3 Güímar

Punta de Güímar

12 Puertito de Güímar

Mirador de Don Martín

TF-1

0   5 km
0   3 miles

Fasnia

10 Porís de Abona

Punta de los Roquetes

Above: A mountain track in the Barranco del Infierno not far from Adeje

Below: The most extraordinary landscape in Tenerife is made up of volcanic peaks and plains

In Three Days

If you're not quite sure where to begin your travels, this itinerary recommends three practical and enjoyable days out in the South, taking in some of the best places to see using the Getting Your Bearings map on the previous page. For more information see the main entries.

Day One

Morning

After taking the pretty approach roads through the Bosque de la Esperanza or up from La Orotava, call in at the **Centro de Visitantes** (Visitors' Centre) at the northern end of the ❶**Parque Nacional del Teide** (➤ 118–123). If coming from the south, stop in at the **Parador de las Cañadas del Teide** (where you can stay the night; below; ➤ 133) to drop your bags off and visit the **Centro de Visitantes** (➤ 119) there. Drive to the base of Mount Teide, where you take the *teleférico* (cable car) up to the top (➤ 120). Back at the base, you can head off for lunch at one of five restaurants near the El Portillo Centro de Visitantes or at the parador.

Afternoon

With the couple of hours of daylight remaining, explore the **Roques de García** (➤ 121) and perhaps also wander as far as the great plain of **Llano de Ucanca**, after which you can retire to the parador for the night.

Day Two

Morning
After breakfast and a morning stroll around the parador, drive through the
Llano de Ucanca and then the pine forests to **6 Vilaflor** (➤ 130), where you
could make a stop. The 12km (7.5-mile) stretch of the TF21 road between
Vilaflor and Granadilla de Abona is narrow, rough and endlessly winding and
drops through pine stands and farming terraces, some in use and others long
abandoned. Looking south, you can make out several small volcanoes. You
could take half an hour to pop into **7 Granadilla de Abona** (➤ 131).

Afternoon
By lunchtime you can be in **2 Los Cristianos** (➤ 124), where you will find
plenty of hotels (book ahead; ➤ 133–134). Have lunch at **Don Armando**
(➤ 135) and devote the rest of the afternoon to relaxing on the beach.

Evening
If you're in the mood for a late night there are plenty of options, especially in
neighbouring **2 Playa de las Américas** (above; ➤ 124).

Day Three

Morning
Having previously booked tickets, make an early start and dedicate the
morning to a walk up the **Barranco del Infierno** (➤ 158–159) from the **Costa
Adeje** (➤ 125), followed by a midday dip back in the resorts. Contain your
hunger and head north, dashing up the motorway to **10 Porís de Abona**
(➤ 132), where you can enjoy lunch and a swim.

Afternoon
Go inland for the winding old Santa Cruz road, stop at **11 Arico** (➤ 132)
and the **12 Mirador de Don Martín** (➤ 132). Visit the **3 Pirámides de Güímar**
(➤ 126–127) and then go to **4 Candelaria** (➤ 128–129) to see the **Basílica de
Nuestra Señora de Candelaria**, dedicated to the island's holy patron, Our Lady
of Candelaria.

❶ Parque Nacional del Teide

Majestic Mount Teide, Spain's highest peak, is lord of Tenerife. The mountain was long held in awe by the island's Guanche inhabitants and still inspires today. It's essential to visit this mountain and the bizarre volcanic landscapes surrounding it – one of Spain's most important national parks and symbol of the spirit of Tenerife.

About 500,000 years old, Mount Teide is an active strato-volcano that has grown in successive eruptions (➤ 22–25) to 3,718m (12,195 feet). All around it are lower volcanic peaks and huge mantles of long frozen lava flows. The arid lunar landscape is so unique that plans to have the area made a national park began in 1934. The Civil War put the idea on hold, but 20 years later it became the third national park to be declared in Spain. The 19sq km (7.5 square mile) area is sub-divided into varying classifications, from no-go zones to areas where limited activity is permitted.

Hikers should follow the marked trails in the national park

PROTECT YOURSELF

The top of Mount Teide is high mountain territory. In winter the temperatures can drop below freezing and, even in summer, especially if there's a strong wind, it can be very cold. Also, conditions change rapidly, so a warm morning can quickly turn to a freezing afternoon. Always take a warm jacket, long trousers and hiking boots, as well as sunglasses, sunblock and a hat.

Check the **weather** before setting out. Cloud cover may be sporadic and frequently only reaches an altitude of around 1,600m (5,248 feet), which is below the level of the park. This *mar de nubes* (sea of clouds) is common in winter and caused by prevailing north winds (*alisios*) that pick up sea moisture on the way and hit the lower slopes of the volcano. Often the cloud cover is restricted to the north. If your luck is truly out the mountain itself may be covered and in winter freezing conditions, snow and ice occasionally lead to access being closed.

Park Approaches

Four roads, all of them pretty, lead from the island's extremities to the national park. From the north you have the choice of taking the forest trail through the **Bosque de la Esperanza** (➤ 76) or winding up the northern flank of the range from La Orotava. At the **Mirador Ayosa**, a lookout point at 2,078m (6,816 feet), you leave the forest and emerge in the bare uplands of the park. From here you pass by the white science-fiction domes of the **Observatorio del Teide** before reaching the El Portillo road junction and the **Centro de Visitantes** (Visitors' Centre). The route from La Orotava also arrives at this junction.

From the south, a particularly windy road heads northwest from Granadilla de Abona to **Vilaflor** (➤ 130), from where it climbs through thick Canary pine forest before reaching the park limits at about 2,200m (7,216 feet). From here the road drops into the **Llano de Ucanca** plain and meets the fourth road, which meanders across in less dramatic fashion from the village of **Chío** in the west.

Visitor Centres

In the **El Portillo Centro de Visitantes** you can take a quick look at the displays explaining volcanoes and the park's surprisingly hardy and varied flora and fauna such as the emblematic *tajinaste rojo* plant, bats, lizards and various raptors that survive in this volcanic landscape. The 15-minute video on volcanoes is worth a look. They also have a small bookstore.

The **Centro de Visitantes de Cañada Blanca** is attached to the *parador* (➤ 133). The displays concentrate on how the people, from the superstitious Guanches to Spanish subsistence farmers, have lived with the sometimes angry volcano.

Pico del Teide

If you do nothing else in the national park, zip up to the top of the mountain (almost) in the **Teleférico** (cable-car). It takes eight minutes to whisk you 1,199m (3,933 feet) up to 3,555m (11,660 feet), only a little way short of the peak.

On a beautiful sunny day you will be able to see across the entire archipelago. As you gaze out over the horizon it's as if you are standing on the roof of the world. On a bad day you might see nothing but the famous "sea of clouds".

Two short walks (Nos 11 and 12) lead you to the **Mirador de la Fortaleza**, which looks north, and the **Mirador de Pico Viejo**, oriented southwest. From the latter you can clearly see the yawning mouth of the Pico Viejo crater. Each path is less than 1km (half a mile) long.

A third walk (No 10) leads to the peak, but you may only make this 700m (2,296-foot) climb (a 180m/590-foot altitude gain) with the relevant permit.

Generally only scientists are allowed to go right to the very top of Mount Teide. If you want to hike to the top you need a permit from the **Oficina del Parque Nacional del Teide** (Calle Emilio Calzadilla 5, 4º, 38002 Santa Cruz de Tenerife, tel: 922/290-129, Mon–Fri 9–2). The permit allows you to the top of the peak (trail No 10) but not into the crater itself. Make sure you take your passport to the permit office and when hiking.

> **The Mount Teide cable-car is a big help if you want to get to the top**

EYES ON THE SKIES

The **Observatorio Astrofísico de Izaña** (no public access) is the lesser known of the Canary Islands' astrophysical research centres (the other one is at the Roque de los Muchachos on La Palma). Run by the Instituto de Astrofísica de Canarias (IAC), the Izaña centre (2,400m/7,872 feet) is dedicated to solar research and Big Bang studies. Some of the most sophisticated telescopes in Europe's astronomical arsenal search the crystal-clear skies above the islands for clues to the Beginning of it All.

Walks in the Park

Apart from the two short strolls to the *miradores* (lookout points) around the top of the mountain and the restricted access climb to the peak (see above), a network of nine marked walking paths spreads across the park. They range from a couple of fairly simple two-hour strolls to the tougher eight-hour hike that takes you from the top station of the Teleférico to Pico Viejo and then down to the TF38 road. This latter hike involves an altitude variation of 1,500m (4,920 feet).

The most popular of the short walks is a simple **3.5km (2-mile) circuit** from the *parador* across the road to the **Roques de García** (walk No 3). These oddly shaped rock formations have been sculpted by the effects of erosion cutting weak stone from the tougher core of what were once volcanic dikes.

The **Roque Chinchado**, which has become something of a symbol for the park and shouldn't be missed, has been eaten away at the base and looks ready to topple over.

A fairly easy half-day walk (No 4; a full day if you have to retrace your steps to reach your transport or the *parador*) is the 16km (10-mile) **Siete Cañadas** hike, which arcs south then southwest from the El Portillo Visitors' Centre to the *parador. Cañadas* are barren plains where temporary lakes form if it rains. This hike stretches through a series of such plains along the inside wall of the Circo de las Cañadas, the enormous semi-circular wall of the ancient crater.

A **more demanding hike** (walk No 7) is the climb from the road to the summit (remember you need a permit to reach the peak itself). The first half of this 8.5km (5.5-mile) hike has a fairly gentle climb, during which you pass *huevos del Teide* (Teide eggs), a spattering of volcanic bombs from past eruptions.

The latter half of the walk is much more challenging (remember that you gain 1,400m/4,592 feet in altitude). Most hikers choose to stay a night in the Refugio de Altavista

Anyone can take the short stroll to the Roques de García

mountain refuge (about two-thirds of the way up and very basic, take your sleeping bag), although you could conceivably do the walk and return with the *teleférico* in the same day (or even take the cable-car up and walk down). Call the refuge (tel: 922/010-440) in advance to be sure of a place. It opens from May to November.

WHAT'S THE BUZZ?
In spring beehives are set up in various parts of the park, continuing a long island tradition that is considered beneficial to the park's flora. The hives (*colmenas*) are signposted and clearly it is not a good idea to get too close!

TAKING A BREAK

You have several eating and drinking options. Five restaurants, all within 2.5km (1.5 miles) of each other, operate around the **El Portillo Centro de Visitantes**. Otherwise, the **Parador** (➤ 133) has a restaurant and cafeteria.

Hardy hikers will be tempted to tackle the long march up to the peak via the Altavista refuge

➕ 177 F3

Centros de Visitantes
🕐 Daily 9–4

Teleférico del Teide
☎ 922/010-445; www.telefericoteide.com 🕐 Daily 9–4 💷 Expensive

PARQUE NACIONAL DEL TEIDE: INSIDE INFO

Top tips Given the height of the mountain, oxygen is in shorter supply than lower down. Elderly people and those with delicate health (especially cardio-vascular problems) should think twice before ascending the mountain.

■ If snowfalls are sufficient in winter it is possible to do a little downhill skiing on the Montaña Blanca, and cross-country skiing along the nearby walking trails.

② Los Cristianos, Playa de las Américas and Costa Adeje

Millions of years ago volcanoes emerged and spewed forth rivers of molten lava that slithered down to the coast. Now a kind of man-made lava of apartments and hotels is reversing the tide, gradually spreading inland from the coast and up the frontline volcanoes.

It's hard to tell where one resort ends and the next one begins

There are several ways of looking at the extraordinary sprawl that comprises what was once a poverty-stricken hamlet (Los Cristianos) and volcanic desert (Playa de las Américas and Costa Adeje). One reaction is horror. A whole jumbled city has been created solely because there is year-round sun – even the beaches had to be either created or helped along. It is a soulless and at times tacky metropolis devoted to Fun.

On the other hand, the place keeps many thousands of sun-starved holidaymakers amused, provides employment and has made use of a part of the island so arid that it was otherwise neither useful nor (to many) especially beautiful. Taken in the right spirit, it can be quite entertaining.

Fishermen still operate out of Los Cristianos

A Place to Find the Sun

The centre of **Los Cristianos** exudes the rhythm of a real town. Away from its two beaches, Playa de Los Cristianos and Playa de las Vistas, the back streets and church square are resolutely Spanish, with local shops and cafés. Ferries to La Gomera and boat tours operate from the harbour.

Playa de las Américas, which has fused with Los Cristianos, is an endless array of hotels and apartments, interrupted by

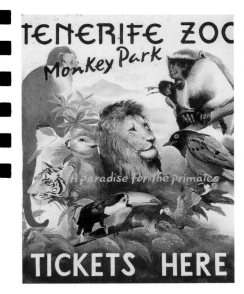

supermarkets, restaurants, bars and clubs. The daytime attraction is the line of virtually identical beaches, protected from ocean surf by sea walls, that runs the length of the resort. A focal point of sorts is the swish **Puerto de Colón** yacht harbour.

Costa Adeje takes up where Playa de las Américas leaves off. Its northernmost end, around **La Caleta** (much of it still under construction), is the classiest effort in the area. Brightly coloured luxury hotels with verdant gardens form a pleasing backdrop to the coast's nicest beaches, especially **Playa del Duque**.

For a break from all the humans, try a visit to the animals at the Tenerife Zoo and Monkey Park

Plenty to Do

Apart from the boat trips and other water-based activities (diving and deep-sea fishing, a yellow submarine and even a pirate ship), various land-based activities have been developed. They include the **Las Águilas Jungle Park**, where you can watch free-flying eagles and condors (➤ 138); the **Parques Exóticos** with a cactus garden, the Amazonia rainforest garden, and animals ranging from iguanas to squirrel monkeys; **Tenerife Zoo and Monkey Park** (primates, lions, crocodiles and other critters); and **Aqualand** (➤ 138) with lots of water slides and a dolphinarium. All are located inland from the resorts which provide free shuttle buses.

■ TAKING A BREAK

If you want to take a break from the general tourist fare, sneak around to the unassuming **Rincón del Marinero** restaurant, opposite the Casa del Mar building behind the port in Los Cristianos (tel: 922/793-553, daily noon–11). The seafood is fresh and well prepared.

✚ 178 A2

LOS CRISTIANOS, PLAYA DE LAS AMÉRICAS AND COSTA ADEJE: INSIDE INFO

Top tip In Los Cristianos there are lots of boat excursions: whale- and dolphin-spotting cruises, trips to the Acantilado de los Gigantes (➤ 102–103) and also cruises around the island.

3 Pirámides de Güímar

For hundreds of years people thought that the strange structures on the edge of Güímar were simply elaborate terraces created by farmers, much like the others you see all over this part of the island. Then along came the late Norwegian anthropologist, Thor Heyerdahl. He came to the conclusion that they were created by men, but many centuries ago and for quite different purposes. In his estimation what you see here is a group of modest step pyramids, built as temples for worshipping the sun.

The **Pirámides de Güímar**, of varying sizes, are like grand platforms. Stairways built into the side allowed worshippers to reach the flat stage at the top of the pyramids in order to pray. Evidence refuting long-held claims that the pyramids were simply farmers' terraces is considerable. While farming terraces are cobbled together with loose rocks, these have been carefully fashioned. The corners and edges have been worked to fit precise rectangular plans.

Celestial Links

The main complex of pyramids was built in such a way that the platforms are orientated toward sunset of the summer

Were the pyramids used for sun worship?

AN ARDUOUS ATLANTIC CROSSING

In the 1930s Thor Heyerdahl, 1914–2002, finished his zoology and geography studies in Norway and set off for a year to study wildlife in the Pacific islands. During this time he came to believe that centuries ago South American tribesmen might have reached Polynesia. The only way they could have done so was in balsa boats, so Heyerdahl had one built and in 1947 sailed it with a crew of five from Callio (Peru) to Raroia in Polynesia. The 8,000km (4,960-mile) trip took 101 days. It was just the beginning. In 1969 and 1970 he had two boats built of papyrus reeds, the Ra I and Ra II (right), which he sailed from Safi (Morocco) to the Caribbean. Thus he showed that it was at least possible that Egyptian mariners had done the same.

solstice. The late Thor Heyerdahl, who proved that ancient mariners may have crossed the Atlantic to the Americas centuries before Christopher Columbus, challenged received wisdom by suggesting there is a link between the pyramidal structures of Egypt, Tenerife and South America.

You can learn how and why Heyerdahl came to these conclusions by visiting the **museum and educational centre** in the **Casa Chacona**. Using pre-Columbian art and other evidence, Heyerdahl asked if foreigners, perhaps from North Africa, came to South America and communicated the ideas behind pyramid building, sun-worship and mummification. If Heyerdahl was right, there is indeed no reason why they might not have called in to the Canary Islands too. A **video** in the auditorium provides further evidence.

TAKING A BREAK

You can get a sandwich and drinks in the **café** at the **Pirámides de Güímar** complex. Or, there are a couple of restaurant/bars a few metres to the left.

➕ 180 B2 ✉ Calle Chacona s/n ☎ 922/514-510; www.piramidesdeguimar.net 🕐 Daily 9:30–6 💶 Expensive

---

PIRÁMIDES DE GÜÍMAR: INSIDE INFO

Top tip Set to one side of the complex is a full size model of the *Ra II*, one of the several reed vessels Thor Heyerdahl built and sailed across the Atlantic. Small-scale models of other modern ocean-going reed boats are also on display.

4 Candelaria

Less than 20km (12.5 miles) south of Santa Cruz, the scruffy coastal town of Candelaria is far more important for what it represents than for what there is to see. If you are here on 15 August, you will witness one of Tenerife's most important fiestas and a pilgrimage of international fame – the Fiesta de Nuestra Señora de la Candelaria (Feast of the Assumption).

Candelaria, a traditional fishing town, is where Tenerife's Guanche past and Spanish present fuse together in an unlikely but popular myth.

The Virgin Mary, who supposedly appeared to the Guanches here as a statue, has formed the centrepiece of Candelaria's life since the earliest days of the Spanish occupation. Night was falling quickly as two Guanche shepherds suddenly found their flock unwilling to proceed near the Chimisay (today Candelaria) beach. They could soon see the problem – a strange woman stood in their path. Attempts to get her to move resulted in the two men wounding themselves and so they ran to inform their chief, the *mencey* of Güímar. He arrived and, when all had realised that the "woman" was actually a miraculous statue that healed the two men, had it moved to a cave of honour.

The grand **Basílica de Nuestra Señora de Candelaria** (Basilica of Our Lady of Candelaria) is the focal point of the town. Characterised by a tall bell-tower (with a curious gallery in the form of a Canarian balcony wrapped round the top) and sturdy, sombre facade, it was completed in 1958, although a church has stood here since around 1530. The statue of the Virgin Mary and murals inside are worth a quick look.

The balcony on top of the Basilica's belfry is a curious architectural detail

Fiesta

Every year enormous crowds of pilgrims flock here for the **Fiesta de**

Nuestra Señora de la Candelaria (Feast of the Assumption) on 15 August (▶ 11). They come from around the islands and as far away as South America to venerate the statue of the Virgin Mary. They say the town authorities decreed the Feast of the Assumption to be the feast also of the Virgin of Candelaria in order to attract more pilgrims over a holiday period. Whatever the truth of this, the real feast day is 2 February, so the faithful have a choice. What they come to venerate has little to do with any image that so baffled the Guanches. The statue, clothed in glorious white and seated on high behind the main altar, was carved in 1827 to replace a predecessor that was whipped away from the church by a freak tidal wave the year before.

More to See

Aside from the Basilica, sights in Candelaria include a parish church and the charming 17th-century **Iglesia de Santa Ana**. Along the waterfront esplanade before the Plaza de la Basílica, in which pilgrims gather on the feast day, stands an intriguing series

The Virgin Mary of Candelaria attracts pilgrims from far and wide of nine outsize statues. These wild and woolly looking men are **Guanche chiefs**, although any accuracy in their representation must be purely accidental. These kings have their backs turned to the Atlantic and a black-sand beach, one of several around Candelaria.

TAKING A BREAK

A good spot to stop for a traditional Canarian lunch is **El Archete** near the Basilica (▶ 136).

✚ 180 C2

Basílica de Nuestra Señora de Candelaria
✉ Plaza de la Basílica 🕐 Daily 7:30–1, 3–7:30 💷 Free

CANDELARIA: INSIDE INFO

Top tips Before rushing off up or down the coast, you might want to dedicate a little time to a wander around the warren of lanes that constitute what there is of the **old town**, up the hill behind the church.
■ The high territory west of Candelaria but within its municipal boundaries is a protected **wildlife area** notable for its pines and other trees.

At Your Leisure

5 Siam Park

Touting itself as the biggest and most spectacular water park in Europe, Siam Park has certainly made a big splash in the press. But there's more to do here than swim – there are water rides including the spectacular Dragon raft ride and the Giant with its centrifugal pool. The 18.5ha (7.5 acre) park also offers lush gardens and animal encounters with playful sea-lions. Styled like a tropical Asian jungle garden, it's a great place to let off steam in the pools. Alternatively you can learn to surf on the artificial waves at the Wave Palace where waves can be programmed to reach 3m in height, or simply laze around enjoying the shady foliage.

There is a range of restaurants and cafés on site and a floating Thai-style market where you can shop for souvenirs.

➕ 178 B2 ✉ Off exit 29 TF1, Playa de las Americas ☎ 922/750-032; www.siampark. net ◷ Mid-Mar to late Oct daily 10–6, late Oct to mid-Mar daily 10–5 💲 Expensive (also combined ticket with Loro Parque)

6 Vilaflor

At 1,160m (3,805 feet), the tranquil farming town of Vilaflor claims to be the highest town in Spain. It's position marks the point at which

The lunar landscape near Vilaflor

the farm terraces that spread south towards the coast begin in earnest. Further up pine stands take over on the way to Mount Teide. On a fine day the views up and down from Vilaflor are good, but the town itself offers only a few curiosities.

At the southern end, on Calle de Santa Catalina, is the **Hotel El Sombrerito**. You can't miss the yellow paint and green timberwork and balcony. A collection of farm implements inside passes for the town's museum, but it's a cosy place to have lunch or stay.

The top of the town is dominated by the single-nave **Iglesia de San Pedro**, built in the shape of a Latin cross. A few steps from this 17th-century church are a former convent and church dedicated to Vilaflor's most famous son, Hermano Pedro (Brother Peter, 1626–67, real name Hernando Pedro de San José Betancourt) who started life as a shepherd in the hills around the town. During his adult life in Tenerife, he went to live in a **cave** (an object of pilgrimage near El Médano, ► 131) before setting off for Guatemala, where he founded the Order of Bethlehem. In 1967

On a narrow coast road 7km (4.5 miles) west of El Médano is the fishing village of Los Abrigos, important to the visitor for the fresh seafood served in its simple waterfront restaurants.

the town set a plaque in the convent recalling his "extraordinary virtues", hindsight that must have the brother turning in his grave.

In 1993 the Guatemalan government added its own pious note of praise by erecting a statue in the steep square below the Iglesia de San Pedro. The father was beatified in 1980 and canonised by Pope John Paul II in 2002. He is the first Canarian to be made a saint.

➕ 178 C3 ✉ 21km (13 miles) south of the parador, Parque Nacional del Teide

⑦ Granadilla de Abona

A typically sleepy interior town, Granadilla is worth a quick detour if you're driving past. Head for the town centre and the **Iglesia de San Antonio de Padua**, with a grey baroque facade and 19th-century bell-tower. Stretching away from the church is the charming little Calle de la Iglesia. Another street that the town council has started to recover from decay is **Calle del Arquitecto Marrero**. To find it, follow Calle del Pino down from the church and it's on your right. The outstanding building here is also a charming *casa rural* (➤ 36) called the Traspatio.

➕ 179 D3 ✉ 23km (14 miles) northeast of Los Cristianos

⑧ Las Galletas and the Costa del Silencio

What little evidence there may once have been of a fishing village at Las Galletas has long been buried in the swathes of holiday apartments and hotels, with the occasional tourist restaurant thrown in. The sprawl

The conditions for windsurfing attract fans from all around the world

is spreading and makes for a dusty, grey mess with a pebble beach. Next around the coast to the west are the slightly more thoughtfully planned holiday resorts of the "Silent Coast". At least there are some trees here.

➕ 178 C1 ✉ 13km (8 miles) southeast of Los Cristianos

⑨ El Médano

The wind howls long and hard off this southeastern point, making the beaches on either side of it great for windsurfing. The beaches are the best natural strands on the island and are comparatively wild and empty, but the town has less to recommend it. Apartment blocks have all but obliterated the original hamlet and stretch back inland, surrounded by the barren land that is a hallmark of the south.

Off the road that connects the town with the TF1 motorway a side road is signposted west to the **Cueva del Hermano Pedro** (➤ 130). The cave, where Hermano Pedro of Vilaflor lived for a while, must be one of the world's oddest places of pilgrimage, at the end of Tenerife Sur Airport's eastern runway. The area around the cave will benefit from more than €1.5 million of beautification and landscaping during 2009 and 2010.

➕ 179 D2 ✉ 22km (13.5 miles) east of Los Cristianos

⑩ Porís de Abona

It would appear that the secret of this once fairly unassuming fishing village is now out. Around the inlet where locals moor their little boats, residential projects are beginning to fill the arid emptiness. Still, the two main reasons for visiting remain valid for the moment.

Porís de Abona has more than its share of straightforward seafood restaurants, making it a good lunch stop en route to somewhere else.

Should you decide to hang about longer, head 1km (0.5 miles) around the bay to **Punta de Abona** for the best beach. Another kilometre or so down the coast is a **lighthouse** where the locals go fishing.

A 1.5km (1-mile) stroll brings you to another small and secluded strand of beach, the **Caleta Maria Luisa**.

➕ 179 F3 ✉ 34km (21 miles) northeast of Los Cristianos

⑪ Arico

A 7km (4.5-mile) drive inland from Porís de Abona, Arico is divided into several parts, of which the most attractive is **Arico Nuevo**, which in spite of its name (New Arico) is the oldest part of town. A narrow street unfolds downhill from the main inland highway, the TF28, lined with charming houses, uniformly whitewashed, with dark green doors and window frames. Halfway along, the street opens up into a peaceful little square, **Plaza de la Luz**, where you'll find the cheerful parish church.

➕ 179 E3 ✉ 6km (3.5 miles) west of Porís de Abona

⑫ Mirador de Don Martín

After a seemingly endless string of hairpin bends in country that just imperceptibly begins to get green, you arrive at the Mirador de Don Martín, one of the best lookout points along the inland highway between Los Cristianos and Santa Cruz. From here you can see north as far as Santa Cruz and across the ocean to the island of Gran Canaria.

➕ 180 B1 ✉ 5km (3 miles) south of Güímar

The parish church of Arico lies at the centre of the surprising colonial village

Where to... Stay

Prices

The following price ranges are for a double room in high season, IGIC sales tax included. Rates vary seasonally.

€ under €70   €€ €70–120   €€€ over €120

PARQUE NACIONAL DEL TEIDE

Parador de las Cañadas del Teide €€€

Tenerife's only *parador* occupies a stunning national-park location at the foot of Mount Teide. Refurbished and upgraded, the hotel merges unobtrusively into the surrounding sandy plains, and picture windows overlook a startling array of weirdly eroded rocks and lava gardens. As darkness falls, this isolated setting is incredibly quiet. Inside, the hotel is comfortably cheerful, with exposed stone and open fires. Rooms are spacious and well equipped. There is a restaurant with traditional food.

🚏 177 E3 🖂 38300 La Orotava
☎ 922/374-841; www.parador.es

PLAYA DE LAS AMÉRICAS AND LOS CRISTIANOS

Aparthotel Panorama €

One of the smaller aparthotel complexes in this part of the island, the 174 units are set in two- and three-storey buildings around the pool. Kitchenettes are basic but the studios and apartments are clean and spacious. There's a laundry

internet café on site. The nearest beach is 300m (330 yards) away.

🚏 178 A2 🖂 Avenida Gran Bretaña
☎ 922/791-611; www.hovima-hotels.com

Jardín Caleta €

A bright modern 5- to 6-storey aparthotel complex that seems to have lots of happy clients. There are almost 250 units in all surrounding a children's playground, swimming pool, TV room and two bars. There's even a tennis court for budding Andy Murrays and a driving range for budding Tiger Woods. The units are spacious and well furnished for the 3-star standard.

🚏 178 A2 🖂 Avenida Las Gaviotas 32, La Caleta ☎ 922/710-976;
www.hovima-hotels.com

Jardín Tropical €€€

The Jardín Tropical feels delightfully secluded. The architecture is a Moorish fantasy of tiles and turrets, domes and arches, while the furnishings and public areas are casual but stylish. Outside, the gardens billow with colourful vegetation. All the rooms are just as charming, in carved wood and wicker. Pools set by the water's edge supplement those in the hotel grounds. There are several exceptional restaurants, and health and fitness treatments to tempt everyone.

🚏 178 A2 🖂 Calle Gran Bretaña s/n, Playa de las Américas ☎ 922/746-000;
www.jardin-tropical.com

Parque Santiago €–€€

This huge complex – the size of a small village – is a family-friendly aparthotel property with good on-site facilities, including an ample choice of casual and fine dining restaurants, a fitness centre, children's adventure park and internet café. The whitewashed accommodation blocks are set in three "parques" around several good-sized pools within the 6.7ha (16 acre) site, giving the feel of different local districts. Apartments have kitchenettes giving you the flexibility of self-catering of you want it.

✛ 178 A2 ✉ Avenida Litoral, Playa de las Américas ☎ 922/746-103; www.parquesantiago.com

Sir Anthony €€€

Describing a gentle crescent just back from the waterfront, the 72 rooms that make up this luxury hotel, built in 1989, are pleasantly unobtrusive. The spacious accommodation is bright, with marble bathrooms and, best of all, a private terrace – ideal for breakfast with ocean views. Immediately fronting the rooms are the pool and gardens, and a quick stroll away is Playa del Camisón.

✛ 178 A2 ✉ Paseo Marítimo s/n, Playa de las Américas ☎ 922/757-545; www.siranthonyhotel.es

COSTA ADEJE

Colón Guanahaní €€–€€€

One of the most attractive hotels in the Fañabe district of Costa Adeje, this well-equipped establishment

has a quiet and relaxing style, even though it is on a fairly busy road. Its colonial-look architecture extends round large freeform seawater pools and tiled sundecks shaded by palms. The spacious, stylish rooms all have balconies.

✛ 178 A2 ✉ Calle Bruselas, Playa de Fañabe ☎ 922/712-046; www.colonguanahani.com

Gran Hotel Bahía del Duque €€€

This luxury complex consists of 20 individual buildings in Mediterranean and Canarian styles. The reception area welcomes with aviaries, fountains and exotic flowers, and within the beautifully kept grounds are turreted accommodation blocks and restaurants. There's direct access to an immaculate beach with an adventurous selection of watersports.

✛ 178 A2 ✉ Calle Alcalde Walter Paetzmann s/n ☎ 922/746-900; www.bahia-duque.com

Sheraton La Caleta Resort & Spa €€€

This magnificent property set in beautifully landscaped grounds is one of the best hotels on Tenerife. With 274 rooms, it's not too crowded, and you're sure to find ample space to relax around one of the three freeform pools (heated in winter). Rooms are spacious and well furnished, and there's a luxurious contemporary Canarian feel in the public areas. The spa is the pièce de resistance covering 1800sq m (20,000sq ft) with massage suites, and a fully equipped gym and fitness suite.

✛ 178 A2 ✉ Calle La Enramada 9, Adeje ☎ 922/162-000; www.starwoodhotels.com

GÜÍMAR

Hotel Rural Finca Salamanca €€–€€€

This charming restored farmhouse in lush gardens attracts visitors for the nearby Pirámides de Güímar. It is set in a peaceful location – 5ha (12

acres) of avocado, mango and citrus groves surround the hotel – and has exceptionally stylish decor. The airy raftered restaurant has Canarian specialities and local wine.

✛ 180 B2 ✉ Carretera Güímar, El Puertito Km 1.5 ☎ 922/514-5 30; www.hotel-fincasalamanca.com

VILAFLOR

El Nogal €€–€€€

The main attraction of this simple place is its location near Vilaflor. Spectacular views stretch to Los Cristianos and the Atlantic. A low-key, cream-washed building, once part of an 18th-century estate, has been sympathetically restored to create a charming hotel. Each of its 29 rooms is different and prettily decorated in traditional Canarian style. Satellite TV and minibars are standard fixtures. The neat gardens surround a pool terrace and the hotel has a new spa complex.

✛ 178 C3 ✉ Camino Real s/n,La Escalona ☎ 922/726-050; www.hotelnogal.com

Where to...
Eat and Drink

Prices

The following price ranges indicate what you can expect to pay per person for a meal, including drinks, tax and tip.

€ under €20   €€ €20–40   €€€ over €40

PLAYA DE LAS AMÉRICAS AND LOS CRISTIANOS

Don Armando €

Amid the touristy parades, this Spanish-looking place adds a very welcome touch of regional authenticity. Beyond the typical bar where Spanish voices can be heard, a spacious terrace restaurant offers grandstand views of the seafront. The all-day menu has several classic tapas dishes.

🚹 178 B2 ⊠ Calle San Telmo, Los Cristianos ☎ 922/796-145 ⓒ Mon–Sat 11:30–4:30, 8–11:30

El Patio €€€

The hotel Jardín Tropical (▶ 133) has several lovely restaurants and this elegant place produces some of the best cooking on the island – and has a Michelin rosette to prove it. Ambitious menus blend Canarian and Spanish cuisine with international flair: a gastronomic version includes seven different dishes to sample, and there's an impressive cellar. The shady terrace dining room is charmingly decorated in blue and white tiles with billowing plants and fountains.

🚹 178 A2 ⊠ Hotel Jardín Tropical, Calle Gran Bretaña s/n, Playa de las Américas ☎ 922/746-000 or 922/746-061 ⓒ Daily 7pm–midnight

Las Rocas €€€

Terraces stretch over the waves at this romantic, chic restaurant attached to one of the resort's top hotel, the Jardín Tropical (▶ 133). Fish and seafood predominate. Rice dishes are another speciality, and there's an extensive list of Canarian wines. Try langostinos al ajillo (king prawns with garlic) or cherne (sea bass). Beyond the rocks that give this place its name, views stretch towards La Gomera. Sunsets are tremendous so it's a good idea to bag a waterfront table if you can.

🚹 178 A2 ⊠ Hotel Jardín Tropical, Calle Gran Bretaña s/n, Playa de las Américas ☎ 922/746-064 ⓒ Daily 1–4, 7–11

La Tasca de mi Abuelo €

A small family-run place with rustic wooden tables and terracotta tiled floors serves an excellent range of tapas and other Spanish dishes. It's always packed with local Canarians. The air-dried ham is sliced as you watch – delicious!

🚹 178 A2 ⊠ CC San Marino, Local 13, Los Cristianos ☎ 922/794-466 ⓒ Tue–Sat noon–4, 8–11, Sun noon–4pm

COSTA ADEJE

El Molino Blanco €€

Although geared mainly towards foreign visitors, the rustic setting and welcoming atmosphere here promise an enjoyable visit. Old wine barrels have been pressed into service as light fixtures, and tables stretch from its attractive dining areas on to large garden terraces with abundant climbing plants and citrus trees. Both the wine list and menu are wide ranging; you may spot unusual items like carne de cabra (goat) or avestruz (ostrich). Why not be adventurous and try something new?

🚹 178 A2 ⊠ Avenida de Austria 5, San Eugenio Alto ☎ 922/796-282 ⓒ Wed–Mon 1pm–midnight

Otelo I €€

Perched by the Barranco del Infierno, Adeje's famous gorge (▲158), this unassuming bar/restaurant does a brisk trade in providing drinks and sustenance to walkers. It serves bar snacks and a variety of popular local dishes like rabbit and *pollo al ajillo* (chicken in either garlic or a spicy *mojo* sauce).

🖽 178 B3 ⊠ Calle Los Molinos 44, Barranco del Infierno, Adeje ☎ 922/780 374 🕔 Wed–Mon 11am–midnight

CANDELARIA

El Archete €€€

Widely regarded as probably Candelaria's best eating place, El Archete is in a traditional old timbered house not far from the main square, where the town's famous pilgrimage church stands. The atmosphere is refined and civilised, complementing its creative repertoire of interesting Canarian dishes. Graceful parlour palms form an archway over the smartly set tables. Specialities include *papas negras rellenas de cherne con salsa de caviar* (black potatoes stuffed with sea bass in caviar sauce).

🖽 180 C2 ⊠ Lomo de Aroba 2, ☎ 922/ 500-115 🕔 Mon, Wed–Sat 1–5.30, 7.30–midnight, Tue 1–5.30

VILAFLOR

El Mirador €–€€

Views over the dramatic mountain scenery near the entrance to the Parque Nacional del Teide are an undeniable advantage of this restaurant, so bring your camera with you. The food isn't bad either, with a wide range of Canarian and international dishes. The restaurant takes its name from a panoramic lookout point (*mirador*) set above the roadside on the outskirts of the village. Most customers head for the terrace tables outside.

🖽 178 C3 ⊠ Ermita de San Roque ☎ 922/709-135 🕔 Sat–Thu 11–8, Sun 12–8; closed May

GRANADILLA DE ABONA

El Jable €€

Accomplished cooking of hearty Canarian fare puts this established bar/restaurant into the top league. The interior walls feature local volcanic stone and dark wood, and wicker lampshades and bright modern paintings decorate. The mainstays are fish and meat, fine cheese and wine. Outstanding dishes include *queso a la plancha con mojo-cilantro* (baked smoked goat's cheese with coriander sauce).

🖽 179 D3 ⊠ Calle Bentejuí 9, San Isidro ☎ 922/390-698; 🕔 Mon 7:30pm–11pm, Tue–Sat 1–4, 7.30–11; closed 15–30 Jun

EL MÉDANO

Perlas del Mar €€

Opinions differ over which is the best of the fish restaurants lining the water's edge at Los Abrigos, but this one has perhaps the best location. Select your fish from the counter and specify how you want it cooked – steamed, grilled or fried. The lack of labels may make the decision between *mero* (grouper), *vieja* (parrotfish) or *salmonetes* (red mullet) a bit tricky, but the staff are happy to help. The tables on the terrace make a fine spot to watch the sun set over the waves.

🖽 178 C1 ⊠ Calle La Marina, Los Abrigos ☎ 922/170-014 🕔 Mon–Sat noon–11; closed 15–30 Sep

Los Roques €€–€€€

Set directly on the coast with a wonderful terrace, Los Roques is a great modern restaurant. A fusion menu features dishes such as tuna tartar, octopus ceviche or foie gras terrine. The chef tries to source as many ingredients as possible from the islands. The salad and vegetables are grown on the owner's farm. There's a good choice of local bottles on the wine list.

🖽 179 D1 ⊠ Calle La Marina 16, Los Abrigos ☎ 922/749-401; www. restaurantlosroques.com 🕔 Tue–Sat 7pm–11pm

Where to...
Shop

SHOPPING CENTRES

Centros comerciales provide a source of tourist entertainment in the resorts of the south coast. Electronic and photographic equipment, perfume, jewellery, leatherware, fashion, sportswear, gifts and cosmetics line the shelves of countless stores in these purpose-built complexes.

MARKETS

Flea-markets colonise a large patch of the Costa Adeje seafront on Thursday and Saturday mornings, and at Los Cristianos near the Hotel Gran Arona on Sunday. The search for a bargain is an irresistible challenge. Artists and street traders use the promenades as a permanent

window display. Avoid anything made of ivory, an illegal import.

CRAFTS

If you're looking for something typically Canarian, head for the older country towns and villages, where **farmer's markets** and **craft fairs** *(ferias de artesanía)* make good hunting grounds. Vilaflor, Fasnia, San Miguel de Abona and Güímar all hold summer fairs.

On the main routes leading up to the Teide National Park, you'll pass several large **craft centres**. There's a good one on the main road at Guía de Isora, north of Costa Adeje. Besides the usual range of embroidery, pottery and wickerwork, look for folk music recordings, local wine and flower perfumes.

Where to...
Be Entertained

NIGHTLIFE

The most frenetic discos, easily detectable by their decibel levels, cluster around the commercial strip known as **Las Veronicas** near Troya beaches. **The Starco** complex on the inland side of the main seafront promenade and **The Patch** towards Los Cristianos throb to a similar beat after dark.

Ephemeral as dragonflies, reputations can easily fade and die within a season. **Bobby's** (Las Veronicas 4), **Bonkers** (Las Veronicas 3) are popular. The current pick of the crop include **China White's** and **The Full Monty** at Las Veronicas 1, **Gaelic Corner** and **Shenanigans** at The Patch, and **Leonardo's**, **Mett** and **Lineker's** at Starco. **Pleasure Island** (www.pleasureislandtenerife.com)

offers evening fun for all the family from crazy golf to video games.

Towards Los Cristianos, the bizarre pseudo-classical **Pirámide de Arona** (Avenida de las Américas s/n, tel: 922/757-549) puts on the most ambitious gala perfomances in the south of Tenerife, including cabaret acts and tasters of flamenco, opera and ballet, or roll the dice at **Casino de las Américas** (tel 922/793-758) in Hotel Gran Tinerfe.

A popular evening excursion advertised in hotels and travel agencies is **Castillo de San Miguel** (San Miguel Aldea Blanca, tel: 922/700-276; www.castillosanmiguel.com), a mock-medieval dinner show of jousting and jollity off the Autopista del Sur. It's good fun and includes some virtuoso feats of horsemanship.

BOAT TRIPS

Many boat trips involve **whale- or dolphin-watching** off the west coast, or a mix of beach parties and leisure cruises. Most trips depart from Puerto Colón (Playa de las Américas) or Los Cristianos, and include snorkelling or scuba diving. **Tropical Delfin** (Pier 12, Puerto Colón, tel: 922/750-085; www. tenerifedolphin.com; daily at 10:15am) is a very conservation-minded whale-watching vessel. *Nostramo* (from Playa San Juan, tel: 922/750-085; daily 10am), a majestic 1918 schooner, sails in style to the cliffs of Los Gigantes. **Glass-bottom** and **submarine boats** have underwater magic, though most marine life stays some way off the churned up waters of these resorts. By far the most popular boat excursion from the southern resorts is to **La Gomera**. Hydrofoils and ferries leave regularly from Los Cristianos. The two main companies are **Fred Olsen** and **Garajonay Exprés**.

ATTRACTIONS

The waterslides and fountains of the popular **Aqualand** (Avenida de Austria, San Eugenio Alto 15, Costa Adeje, tel: 922/715-266, www.aqualand.es; daily 10–6) provide an unexpected oasis at San Eugenio. Children just love it!

One of the area's most popular visitor attractions is **Las Águilas Jungle Park** (Carretera Los Cristianos-Arona, Km 3, tel: 922/729-010; www. aguilasjunglepark.com; daily 10–5:30 (last ticket 4:30), flying shows at noon and 4pm, expensive), a bird park where eagles and falcons display aeronautical feats amid some jungle-like vegetation.

OUTDOOR PURSUITS

Many resort hotels have impressive leisure facilities including **beach clubs** and **tennis courts** that non-residents can pay to use.

Bicycle hire is available in all the major resorts.

Watersports

Puerto Colón and Los Cristianos harbour are the best starting points for **deep-sea fishing**, yacht charter, sea-scooters and pedaloes. Watersports are advertised on local beaches, including **jetskiing** and **parascending**. **Scuba diving** centres operate in all the main resorts; the clear, rock-lined waters of the Costa del Silencio are a rewarding location. If **windsurfing** is your thing, head for El Médano. The strong prevailing trade winds (*alisios*) provide some of the best conditions in the world. Sailboard hire and tuition are available on the main beaches; try Playa Sur (tel: 922/176-688).

Golf

Golf del Sur (Urb. Golf del Sur, San Miguel de Abona, tel: 922/738-170; www.golfdelsur.net) has exotic palms and cacti amid bunkers of black sand. **Amarilla Golf** (Urb. Amarilla Golf, San Miguel de Abona, tel: 922/730-319; www.amarillagolf. es) has a superb oceanside setting and

a pitch-and-putt course and practice driving range. The newly developed **Golf Costa Adeje** (Finca Los Olivos s/n, Adeje, tel: 922/710-000; www. golfcostaadeje.com) looks over the sea towards La Gomera. It has 27 holes.

Flower Spotting

To remind yourself what natural scenery looks like, head for Adeje's **Barranco del Infierno** (▶ 158), a cactus-filled ravine ending in a waterfall. Note that the gorge is only open to 200 people per day, so visitors are advised to book ahead (tel: 922/782-885). Allow 3–4 hours and take plenty of drinking water.

Make for **Siete Cañadas** (▶ 121) in early summer to see the flamboyant *tajinaste rojo* in full bloom, its red-hot-poker spires rearing 2m (6.5 feet) above the cinderbeds of Mount Teide's crater. Many typical plants of these volcanic lands can be seen growing in protected conditions at the **El Portillo Visitor Centre** (▶ 119), or around **Los Roques** (▶ 121) and the *parador* (▶ 133).

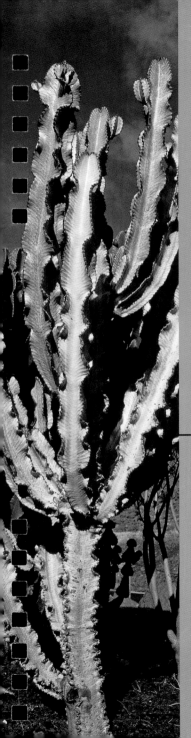

La Gomera

Getting Your Bearings

Just 40 minutes by jetfoil off the southwest coast of Tenerife, La Gomera is known to its 17,000 inhabitants as La Isla Redonda (The Round Island). Measuring 25km (15 miles) by 23km (14 miles), it is the second smallest in the archipelago. About 10 per cent of the island's centre is taken up by the Parque Nacional de Garajonay, an extraordinary mix of frequently mist-enveloped laurel forest and other vegetation culminating in the Garajonay peak.

La Gomera attracts two kinds of tourism: fast one-day tours from Tenerife and a smaller, nature-loving crowd who stay for several days. Walking is becoming increasingly popular and trails abound.

A web of *barrancos* (gorges) spreads from Garajonay to the coast. Much of the island, especially the north and west, is terraced for agriculture (bananas remain the predominant crop), but farmers have always had a tough time of it because of the rugged geography and generally poor soil.

Most boats arrive in the little capital of San Sebastián on the east coast. Two roads head west, one sweeping north through a series of picturesque villages, some with tiny beaches. It then swings southwest into the pretty Valle Gran Rey, a fertile valley of farm terraces that ends in a cluster of beachside villages. The other road proceeds through the Parque Nacional de Garajonay and also links up with the Valle Gran Rey. A couple of roads zigzag south to the Playa de Santiago, which hosts dive schools and a handful of beaches.

Punta de los Órganos

Punta del Peligro

Tamargada 2

Vallehermoso 2

Epina

Macayo

Alojera

Arure

Parque Nacional de Garajonay 4

Las Hayas

TF-713

El Cercado

Valle Gran Rey 3

Chipude

1487 Garajonay

1241 Fortaleza

La Calera

Igualero

Vueltas

Alajeró

La Dama 6 6 **La Rajita**

Punta Falcones

Modest houses squat in among the palms and
farming terraces along the Valle Gran Rey

Laja del Infierno

TF-711 **2 Agulo**

Las
Rosas □
□ Santa Catalina

Las Casas □ **2**
Hermigua

1065 **5**
Encherada **Parque Naturel
de Majona**

Punta Majona

TF-711
Punta Gaviota

Chejelipes
Punta Llana

Casas de Langrero □
Punta de Avalo

Vegaipala □ TF-713
**San Sebastián
de la Gomera**
7 **1**
Benchijigua

Las □
Toscas

Punta Gorda

La ✈
Gomera □ Laguna de
Santiago *Punta Gaviota*
8 Playa de Santiago

0 ——— 5 km
0 ——— 3 miles

A stone parish church marks
the centre of Vallehermoso, a
town in the north of the island

Page 139: Cactus growing in the Valle
Gran Rey

Left: On the beach near Vueltas in the
Valle Gran Rey

★ Don't Miss

At Your Leisure

In Three Days

If you're not quite sure where to begin your travels, this itinerary recommends three practical and enjoyable days out in La Gomera, taking in some of the best places to see using the Getting Your Bearings map on the previous page. For more information see the main entries.

Day One

Morning
Get the first **jetfoil** from Los Cristianos in southern Tenerife for the 40-minute ride across to the modest capital, **❶ San Sebastián** (➤ 144). After organising car hire, head off on a brief stroll around the colonial town where you can see what is supposedly the house where Columbus lodged prior to setting off on his first voyage of discovery. Sit down for a light lunch at one of the waterfront cafés – Casa del Mar (➤ 154) has traditional Canarian dishes.

Afternoon
Set off on a driving tour of the **❷** north of the island (➤ 145–146). Stop at **Hermigua** (➤ 145), where you can take a walk to El Cedro. The pretty drive continues to the coast and then west, where things get a little wilder. **Vallehermoso** (➤ 145) is a handy spot to stop for a drink and, if you stay on, a base for walks. As the road swings south take the turn to **Alojera** (➤ 146) before returning to the main road and descending the **❸ Valle Gran Rey** (below; ➤ 147–149), an ideal spot to spend a couple of nights.

Day Two

Morning
Join whale-watching boat trips or an excursion to **Los Órganos** (above, ➤ 149), the bizarre cliffs in the north of the island. Or alternatively, take a break from travelling and relax on the beach.

Afternoon
After lunching in one of the restaurants at Vueltas, or Charco del Conde in Valle Gran Rey (➤ 155), head up to **Chipude** (➤ 149) to undertake a rewarding walk back south through gorges and past country chapels to the beach at **La Calera**.

Day Three

Morning
Drive east into the **4 Parque Nacional de Garajonay** (➤ 150–151), where you can make a quick ascent of the Alto de Garajonay and see birds like the blue tit, or take a longer walk such as to El Cedro. Enjoy a lunchtime picnic in La Laguna Grande (➤ 151).

Afternoon
Drive south to **6 La Dama and Playa de La Rajita** (➤ 152) for a look at the Atlantic, or go on a southern circuit via **Alajeró** to **8 Playa de Santiago** (➤ 152), where you could swim and eat before heading north to the San Sebastián road to return to the capital in time for the last boat back to Los Cristianos. If you have more time, **diving** (right) is an option in Playa de Santiago. Or stay in a country house in the pleasant district of **7 Benchijigua** (➤ 152).

❶ San Sebastián

A scattering of sights and traditional houses and the occasional market make the obligatory arrival in San Sebastián a pleasant stop.

San Sebastián

The **Torre del Conde** (Count's Tower) was the first building erected by the Spaniards in San Sebastián, in 1447. La Gomera's first lady, Beatriz de Bobadilla, holed up here during the islanders' revolt in 1488 and Christopher Columbus stayed in the **Casa de Colón** (Calle Real 56) before setting out on his voyage of discovery. Today it is a charming colonial house with a courtyard and a smattering of Peruvian artefacts that are just about worth a visit. About 100m (110 yards) closer to the port, the **Iglesia de la Virgen de la Asunción** has a mural depicting the defeat of English pirates on the island in 1743.

Wander through the streets of San Sebastián to get a feel of the town

Last Stop Before the Unknown

Three caravels under the command of Christopher Columbus called in at San Sebastián en route from Spain to take on provisions in mid-August 1492. Columbus was determined to find a western route to the Indies and prove, along the way, that the Earth was round. Legend says he enjoyed a dalliance with Beatriz de Bobadilla, onetime lover of King Ferdinand of Spain and now widowed after the death of her nasty husband.

TAKING A BREAK

The **Casa del Mar** (➤ 154) or the parador (➤ 153) in San Sebastián are both good places to find refreshment.

➕ 185 E3

San Sebastián Tourist Information
✉ Calle Real 4 ☎ 922/870-281 🕘 Mon–Sat 9–1:30, 3:30–6, Sun 10–1

2 Villages of the North

Setting out across the north of the island is a real pleasure, taking in villages like Hermigua and Vallehermoso. The treat is in the travel itself as much as the destination, passing as it does through continually changing countryside and farmland.

The fruit of vine grows around Hermigua

As you head out of San Sebastián along the TF711, you will find yourself quickly submerged in rural La Gomera. The drive is exhilarating, if windy at times. The first village of any substance is **Hermigua**, where you can stop to stretch your legs and get a drink and a snack. From here you can walk for 2–3 hours south to reach **La Boca del Chorro waterfall** – ask for the trail to El Cedro (where there is a camping ground).

To the north, the nicest beach is **Playa de la Caleta**, along a dirt trail that is driveable when dry. The main road winds past the coastal villages of **Agulo** and **Lepe**, which also have

pleasant beaches, before twisting inland to **Tamargada** and **Vallehermoso**. The former is an attractive rural hamlet, while the latter, somewhat larger, makes a handy base for walkers with accommodation and a couple of places to get something to eat.

The road continues south through high ground and the occasional village. Dirt roads lead to the isolated hamlets of **Tazo** and **Arguamul**. A 1km (0.5-mile) walk away from Aguamul is **Playa del Remo** which offers a chance to see something quieter. Further south, a side road makes for a spectacular drive downhill to **Alojera**, which has a tiny beach.

Across the town of Agulo is Mount Teide in its "sea of clouds"

TAKING A BREAK

In the north, **El Silbo** in Hermigua (➤ 155) makes a convenient place to stop during your exploration of the north.

Vallehermoso ⊞ 184 C4
Tamargada ⊞ 184 C5
Agulo ⊞ 185 D4
Hermigua ⊞ 185 D4

VILLAGES OF THE NORTH: INSIDE INFO

Top tips Strangely, the **Parque Nacional de Garajonay's** visitor centre is on the TF711 road between Agulo and Tamargada (follow signs for Las Rosas).
■ About 3km (2 miles) north of Las Rosas is a fine *mirador* (lookout point) over Agulo and the ocean.

Hidden gem If you like secluded coves, walk two hours southwest from San Sebastián to the hamlet of **El Cabrito**. The palm-backed black beach is pretty. Bring food and water.

❸ Valle Gran Rey

A majestic, palm-studded gorge sculpted by farmers who, through the years, have eked out a living growing bananas and tomatoes sweeps down the west side of La Gomera to a huddle of pleasant villages and beaches. The farm terraces look in the distance like enormous natural stairways to heaven. Long ago "discovered" by Germans in search of low-profile tourism, it remains a pleasingly laid-back location.

Farm terraces climb the Valle Gran Rey

The "Valley of the Great King", named after a Guanche ruler, Orone, opens out into a delta as it reaches the coastal settlements of La Calera, La Playa and Vueltas. As you approach the valley from the north, stop at the *mirador* at Arure. From here there are views across the west of the island and over the ocean to the westernmost islands of the archipelago, La Palma (to the north) and El Hierro.

Giant Steps

The road winds down steeply past hamlets, farms and palm stands as you drop into the *barranco* (gorge). The impressive gorge walls, up to 800m (2,624-feet) high, protect the valley from ocean winds, helping to make it the most agriculturally prosperous area on the island.

The fine black sand of **La Playa** makes it the most pleasant beach, although several smaller ones are dotted along the coast on either side of it. A trail leads north to **Playa del Inglés**, while trails to the south of Vueltas go to **Playa de Argaga** and **Playa de las Arenas**.

Of these hamlets, the most intriguing is **Vueltas**, with hilly

Playa Calera is one of several modest beaches at Valle Gran Rey

Opposite: The first sight of Valle Gran Rey takes the breath away

lanes studded with small lodgings, restaurants and bars.

Activities and Excursions

Apart from the beach, the main aquatic activities include **boat trips** to the cliffs of **Los Órganos** (➤ 156). They generally leave at 10:30am and include lunch. Weather permitting, you may see dolphins and whales along the way. Another possibility is to go **diving** or **snorkelling**. Fisch & Co (Calle Lepanto, tel: 922/805-688) organise dives.

Away from the coast, the big attraction is **walking**. Just leaving the road and wandering into the farming hamlets is a treat – you can quickly lose yourself in the tropical farmland, laced with irrigation ditches and dense with sweet tropical odours.

A popular option is to catch the San Sebastián bus to the inland town of **Chipude**, below the southern flank of the Parque Nacional de Garajonay. From there are numerous walking options. A good three-hour round trip takes you on a return journey from Chipude to the grand rocky outcrop known as **La Fortaleza** ("the fort"). From Chipude you could also follow minor ravines southwest past a couple of *ermitas* (little country chapels) and then down the Valle Gran Rey to **La Calera**, a delightful walk of about 3.5 hours.

TAKING A BREAK

Try **Casa Maria** for the famed *papas rellenas* (potato balls stuffed with meat or fish).

✚ 184 B3

VALLE GRAN REY: INSIDE INFO

Top tips Just 4km (2.5 miles) north of Vallehermoso is the dramatic cliff face known as **Los Órganos**. To see this stunning natural wonder you need to arrive by sea. Trips are organised by a couple of companies in Valle Gran Rey (➤ 156).

■ The Club del Mar in Vueltas (tel: 922/805-759) conducts **marine research** and they like to share their knowledge. You can go on four-hour **whale-spotting boat trips** with the club (€27 per person).

④ Parque Nacional de Garajonay

To enter this national park, which covers about 10 per cent of the centre of the island, is to travel millions of years into the past. The *laurisilva* (laurel forest) that is protected here is among the most ancient forests on the planet and one of the few to escape the devastation caused by the last Ice Age. It is topped by the Garajonay peak (1,487m/4,877 feet), from where there are views of Tenerife's Mount Teide and beyond.

UNESCO World Heritage Site

Often enveloped in swirling mists that defy the sand-and-sun impression most people have of the Canary Islands, the lichen- and moss-covered trees in the Parque Nacional de Garajonay, apart from the laurels, constitute hundreds of species. The mist produced by the clash of moist trade winds with warmer breezes from the Sahara causes as much, and sometimes more, precipitation than rain on the island. The ancient tree canopy is so thick that little or no sun penetrates, which explains the lack of other vegetation on the forest floor. In all, wandering about in here can be an eerie experience. The whole area was designated a UNESCO World Heritage Site in 1986.

The *laurisilva* on La Gomera is one of Earth's most ancient forests

Ups and downs in the Parque Nacional de Garajonay

Walking Country

The TF713 road from San Sebastián runs through the middle of the park and passes close to the **Alto de Garajonay** (Garajonay peak, 1,487m/ 4,877 feet). You can get the No 1 bus from San Sebastian and get off at the Pajarito stop, leaving you with about an hour's hike to the top of the peak. It is a fairly easy and popular walk. If you come by taxi or hire car, you can park at the El Contadero pass, from where a 1.5km (1-mile) trail leads to the Alto. On a clear day the views from the top can be magnificent. Apart from the obvious Mount Teide, you can also make out La Palma and El Hierro to the west and sometimes Gran Canaria. Plenty of other **walks** through the park are possible. You can get more information on them from the park's information centre, strangely located north of the park near Agulo. There is another small information booth at La Laguna Grande (➤ below).

From the El Contadero pass a fine walk heads north through the thick **Bosque del Cedro** (cedar wood), although there are few cedars to be seen. The walk is well marked and signposted. You can stop in **El Cedro**, about two hours' walk away. From here you can visit the nearby **Boca del Chorro waterfall** (best in winter).

TAKING A BREAK

You could opt for a picnic at **La Laguna Grande**, a clearing about 3km (2 miles) northwest along the road from the Alto de Garajonay. It has a playground, barbecue grills and a café.

➕ 184 C3

Parque Nacional de Garajonay Visitor Centre
➕ 185 D4 ✉ At Juego de Bolas near Agulo off the north coast road
☎ 922/800-993 🕐 Daily 9:30–4:30

PARQUE NACIONAL DE GARAJONAY: INSIDE INFO

Top tips When walking remember that within the boundaries of the national park you **may not camp nor light fires**.
■ Don't leave any litter behind.
■ Bring **warm and weatherproof gear** as it can be surprisingly cold and you could easily be caught in brief spells of rain.

At Your Leisure

5 Parque Naturel de Majona

Over one third of the area of La Gomera is under some kind of protection order. Majona Park covers swathes of the island northwest of San Sebastian. This is Canarian heath and pastureland, which has been shaped by man, and where you can still see traditional shepherding taking place.

➕ 185 E3

6 La Dama and Playa de La Rajita

The narrow serpentine road to La Dama from the south flank of the Garajonay National Park passes through hamlets like El Cercado and Chipude. Apart from the banana plantations, La Dama offers the spectacular sight of sheer cliffs plunging deep into the Atlantic. A steep trail leads down to the black beach of Playa de la Rajita.

➕ 184 B2 ✉ About 27km (16.5 miles) south of Valle Gran Rey

7 Benchijigua

Benchijigua is a collection of attractive hamlets in southern La Gomera. Some long-abandoned houses have been restored as holiday apartments and make a pleasant rural base for walks into the Parque Nacional de Garajonay.

➕ 184 C3 ✉ About 20km (12.5 miles) west of San Sebastián

8 Playa de Santiago

The fishing town of Playa de Santiago lies on arid land in the island's southeast. For a long time the closest La Gomera came to an industrial centre, with its fish-canning factories and port facilities, Playa de Santiago is trying to reinvent itself as a tourist centre with a luxury hotel and the nearby airport. Sunshine is virtually guaranteed year-round and there's a handful of pleasant black-sand beaches. Playa de Santiago is also a

A quiet corner at Playa de Santiago

launch pad for diving excursions off the island.

➕ 185 D2 ✉ About 25km (15.5 miles) southwest of San Sebastián

---

THEY AIN'T WHISTLING DIXIE

Confronted by the difficult terrain of their island, the Guanches found it easier to whistle messages across the gorges to their neighbours than walk and talk. They developed a kind of morse code known as *el silbo gomero* (Gomeran whistle) that could be heard 4km (2.5 miles) away. Placing their fingers in their mouths and cupping their hands, the islanders created an alphabet – studies have identified almost 3,000 whistled words. Until recently only a few elderly folk could still give this kind of whistle, but it has now been made a compulsory subject in schools.

Where to…
Stay

Prices
The following price ranges are for a double room in high season, IGIC sales tax included. Rates vary seasonally.

€ under €70   €€ €70–120   €€€ over €120

Tourism has increased hugely on La Gomera during the past decade. Now La Gomera's more enterprising and independently minded visitors have a choice of simple but stylish small hotels and *casas rurales* scattered throughout the island, as well as the major resorts. Some cater for walkers.

SAN SEBASTIÁN

Parador de la Gomera €€€
San Sebastián's *parador* stands high above the port up a steeply winding road. The building is a convincing modern copy of a 16th-century convent. Low-rise wings in local stone and dark wood surround the shady courtyards and the furnishings are typically Castilian. Canarian specialities like *vieja* (parrotfish) with *mojo* (spicy sauce) and flambéed bananas feature on the menu in the stately dining room. The subtropical clifftop garden command views over the town and the local coast, with Mount Teide visible on Tenerife.

🚹 185 E3 ☒ Calle Orilla del Llano 1 ☎ 922/871-100; www.paradores.com

VALLEHERMOSO

Tamahuche €
Just outside Vallehermoso's centre, this small hotel makes for a tranquil getaway. The 10 spacious bedrooms all have two generous single beds side by side in rooms of pleasing simplicity. Dark timber floors match the wooden furniture and some of the top floors have an exposed timber ceiling. Straightforward whitewash brings out the contrast and walls of exposed local stone add warmth to public areas like the dining room.

🚹 184 C4 ☒ Calle La Hoya 20 ☎ 922/801-176; hoteltamahuche@ecoturismocanarias.com

HERMIGUA

Hotel Villa de Hermigua €
This 120-year-old complex tumbles down a hillside, with nine double rooms on several levels around a small sunny courtyard. There's a sunroom and TV room. The whole is brought together by the pastel colour scheme. Rooms are prettily decorated in local style and there's a characterful rustic breakfast room filled with antique nick-knacks. From the comfy chairs in the courtyard you can take in the panorama of the surrounding hills.

🚹 185 D4 ☒ Carretera General 117, Hermigua ☎ 922/880-771; www.ecoturismocanarias.com

Ibo Alfaro €€
This delightful rural hostelry is especially popular with groups of walkers. It's a stylish little place on a quiet track above the main street. The cream-painted building dates from the 19th century, and once belonged to a prominent local family. In 1996 it was skilfully renovated in typical Canarian style using natural stone and timber. The interior is cosy, with darkwood furnishings and lots of personal touches. Breakfast is served on a sun terrace with lovely views.

🚹 185 D4 ☒ 38820 Hermigua ☎ 922/880-168; www.ecoturismocanarias.com/iboalfo

Where to...
Eat and Drink

Prices

The following price ranges indicate what you can expect to pay per person for a meal, including drinks, tax and tip.

€ under €18   €€ €18–36   €€€ over €36

VALLE GRAN REY

Jardín del Conde €€

Three low-rise, pastel-coloured blocks in Mediterranean style surround a large, freeform pool terrace on the landward side of Valle Gran Rey's seafront road. Behind the hotel loom dramatic terraced hills.

This attractive apartment complex has relatively limited public areas and facilities, but the site is tidily kept and brightly landscaped with plenty of greenery and flowering plants. Individual apartments (all with one bedroom and a balcony or terrrace overlooking the pool gardens) are light and simple in streamlined, colourful, contemporary style with American-look kitchens. You can hire a satellite TV.

A useful and separately managed mini market and bar stocking all the usual necessities are located near the basement entrance.

➕ 184 B3 ⬜ Avenida Marítima s/n ☎ 922/806-008; www.jardindelconde.com

PLAYA DE SANTIAGO

Jardín Tecina €€€

This imaginative modern complex comprises low-rise, local-style units in an extensive village-like setting in the arid cliffs on the south side of the island.

The former fishing community near by has expanded with the advent of tourism, but Playa de Santiago is still an isolated location offering a well-cushioned retreat. The facilities are excellent and there's a wide range of entertainment and excursions. Yet the ambience is peaceful and relaxing, amid beautiful grounds and the five inviting pools.

There are five restaurants, offering buffets and barbecues. Each has a different feel: gardens, pools or views of the distant ocean. A lift transports you to a beach club on the seafront, where watersports are on offer.

➕ 185 D2 ⬜ Playa de Santiago ☎ 922/145-850; www.jardin-tecina.com

SAN SEBASTIÁN

Casa del Mar €–€€

Nautical photos decorate this airy bar/restaurant. There's a large menu of seafood, attracting a loyal band of local custom. Try the *cazuela* (fish stew) with *gofio* and herbs.

➕ 185 E3 ⬜ Avenida Fred Olsen 2 ☎ 922/870-320 🕐 Mon–Sat 1:30–4, 7:30–10:30

Parador de la Gomera €€–€€€

Non-residents are welcome to dine at La Gomera's attractive national *parador*, though it is advisable to book ahead. The dark-wood dining room overlooks the gardens and the ocean below. Gomeran specialities feature on the menu.

➕ 185 E3 ⬜ Calle Orilla del Llano 1 ☎ 922/871-100 🕐 Daily 11:30–3:30, 7:30–11:30

LAS ROSAS

Las Rosas €€

Panoramic views are a major attraction of this roadside restaurant on the edge of a ravine. It's a popular stop off for groups doing island tours, and is often booked up for set lunches. Food is typically Canarian.

Demonstrations of La Gomera's strange whistling language (*el silbo*, ▶ 152) draw the crowds.

🕀 184 C4 ⊠ Carretera General 🕿 922/800-916 🕔 Daily noon–3:30

HERMIGUA

El Silbo €

This modest bar/restaurant has a flower-decked terrace and is a charming spot to enjoy an inexpensive drink or meal with a view. They do simple Spanish fare, with tapas-style dishes and a fish of the day. It's named after the whistling language of La Gomera (▶ 152).

🕀 185 D4 ⊠ Carretera General 103 🕿 922/880-304 🕔 Daily 1:30–3:30, 7–11:30

AGULO

El Tambor €–€€

A handy choice beside the Garajonay National Park Visitor Centre near Agulo, this rustic bar/restaurant serves appetising Gomeran specialities like *sopa de berros* (watercress soup). Combine a snack with a visit to the centre, with its folk museum, craft displays and a video presentation on the park.

🕀 185 D4 ⊠ Agulo 🕿 922/800-709 🕔 Mon–Sat 11–6

VALLE GRAN REY

Restaurante Abraxas €–€€

This German-owned restaurant adds a bright, modern menu to the traditional offerings on the island. Meats and fish are teamed together with fruits to create innovative taste combinations. There's also a good choice for vegetarians. You can drop in for a late breakfast or a coffee and one of a delicious range of home-cooked cakes. Live music and football are also on offer.

🕀 184 B3 ⊠ Calle el Molino 1, La Puntilla 🕿 922/806-246; www.abraxas-la-gomera. com 🕔 Oct–Mar Mon–Wed, Fri, Sun 10–2, 7–midnight; Sat 10am–midnight; Apr–Sep Mon–Wed, Fri, Sun 5pm–midnight, Sat 2pm–midnight

Where to... Shop

Crafts and food specialities are the main things to buy. Craft centres and workshops are scattered around the island in rural locations as well as the main resorts. San Sebastián supplies little more than basics to the regular tides of visitors from Tenerife. The daily market on Avenida de Colón (Mon–Sat morning) is worth a visit for crafts and farm produce.

CRAFTS

For an overview of La Gomera's traditional wares, call in at the **Parque Nacional de Garajonay Visitor Centre** (Juego de Bolas, near Agulo, tel: 922/800-993), where textiles, musical instruments (tambourines and castanets), baskets made from banana leaves and woodwork are on display.

A craft workshop in Hermigua, **Los Telares** (tel: 922/880-781), specialises in local woven goods, especially hand-made rugs.

The villages of **Chipude** and **El Cercado** to the west of the Parque Nacional de Garajonay are well known for **pottery**, made in the traditional Guanche style without a wheel and fired with a coating of red clay. You can watch it being made in roadside potteries.

Valle Gran Rey has for a long time been an attractive base for expatriate New Age settlers in search of alternative lifestyles. Some make a living from painting and other artistic ventures, so there's also a range of non-indigenous souvenirs on sale around here.

Where to...
Be Entertained

MILK AND HONEY

The process of making *queso de cabra* (goat's cheese), a Gomeran speciality, is explained in the Parque Nacional de Garajonay Visitor Centre's folk museum. You'll find **farm cheeses** on sale at market stalls – buy some freshly baked bread as well and you have an ideal picnic for those energetic walks through the hills.

Another island product is **miel de palma** (palm honey), the sweet, sticky sap tapped from local date-palms. It can be spread on bread like ordinary honey, or used as a topping for pancakes and ice-cream. Small, attractively packed bottles make unusual presents.

Some of the fertile terraces of Valle Gran Rey are planted with **exotic fruits** such as avocados, mangos and pawpaws, on sale at local farms and roadside stalls.

Interesting **wines** are produced on La Gomera too, especially around Agulo and Vallehermoso.

Swap Tenerife's concrete jungles for a unique natural ecosystem of buckled barrancos and primeval forests in the **Parque Nacional de Garajonay.**

WALKING

For more information on walking in the Parque Nacional de Garajonay, call in at the **Visitor Centre** (at Juego de Bolas near Agulo off the north coast road, tel: 922/800-993; daily 9:30–4:30). Trails through the laurel forest start at La Laguna Grande and El Cedro, and free guided walks are organised once a week. Maps can be bought at the visitor centre or in San Sebastián and Valle Gran Rey.

Outside the park, many other excellent **hikes** are possible, though the steep gradients make some of them very taxing. Contact the local tourist office for details.

LA GOMERA'S WHISTLING

Demonstrations of the strange whistling language known as *el silbo gomero* (▶152) are laid on for visitors in popular tourist haunts such as Las Rosas near Vallehermoso (▶154).

BEACH LIFE

All La Gomeran **beaches** are black sand and most are stony, but at intervals around the main northern circuit route, steep tracks trickle down to pretty bays and fishing villages where you can while away a peaceful hour or two. The beaches at Valle Gran Rey (▶147) and **Playa de Santiago** (▶152) are the most developed for tourism, with a few watersports. The **Hotel Jardín Tecina** (▶154) has its own beach club with a pool and dive school.

BOAT TRIPS

From various points, excursion boats depart to inspect the closely packed basalt columns of **Los Órganos** off the north coast, named for their resemblance to organ pipes. Visible only from the sea, these slender hexagonal formations rise 80m (262 feet) from the waterline. The nearest departure point is Puerto de Vallehermoso, but trips also start from Playa de Santiago, Valle Gran Rey and San Sebastián.

Whale-watching, fishing and **sailing trips** are advertised from Vueltas (Valle Gran Rey). Choose a calm day as the waters around La Gomera are notoriously uncomfortable, and boats don't run in rough weather.

Walks and Tours

1 EL BARRANCO DEL INFIERNO

Walk

DISTANCE approx 6.3km/4 miles (return) **TIME** 1.5 hours ascent and 1 hour descent, plus time to look around and enjoy the waterfall **START/END POINT** Restaurante Otelo I, in the upper part of Adeje ⊞ 178 B3

In spite of the fear-inspiring name, the Barranco del Infierno (Hell's Gorge) is actually a fairly easy and popular trek. Tenerife has no rivers and water drains away down the island's many *barrancos*. The cascade that marks the end of this walk meant an assured water supply – a rare boon on the island that led the Guanche chief Tinerfe to make his capital, Adeje, here. The Spaniards followed suit and converted the native village into one of their earliest settlements.

1–2

The trail starts off to the right just behind the **Restaurante Otelo I** (➤ 136; a good spot with balconies and great views where you can have lunch on your return). At this level the terrain is dry and the vegetation dominated by cactus and spurge. The trail, paved in parts, ascends slowly and follows the contours of the left side of the *barranco*. After 15 minutes or so the path swings left and then right in an upward hairpin bend, at the end of which

you reach the first of several lookout points. Here you are high above the gorge floor and the views back down to Adeje are impressive.

2–3

Turn your back on the town and proceed. For the next 10 minutes you climb slowly and reach another *mirador* (lookout point), this time affording views deeper into the gorge, before the trail swings sharp left and then right again to follow the wall.

3–4

Next you cross a man-made channel that carries some of the water downhill. By the time you re-cross it seven minutes on, the trail dips down to the gorge floor. As you descend, the walls seem to loom ever higher. The cactus and spurge can still be seen higher up, but you are now walking amid a greater variety of greenery. You soon start to climb again and a quick right then left along the narrowing and muddy path bring you to a little cascade, **La**

The rapidly changing scenery along the *barranco* leads the way to a cool waterfall

Cojedora. From now on you are accompanied by the sound of running water and a growing medley of insects and birds. The vegetation crowds the trail and at times forms brief green tunnels – watch out for the prickly undergrowth on bare legs and the pretty rose-coloured Canary bell-flowers.

4–5

You are now in the prettiest and steepest stretch of the walk. You cross and re-cross the stream several times as you wind your way up. Several curves in the course of the gorge are deceptive – just when you think the end is in sight you turn and see there is more ahead. But then the end comes abruptly. After about 1.5 hours of walking the trail turns right and suddenly, before you, the canyon walls shut off further progress. A blissful waterfall plunges into a clear pool at the base of the rocky wall. Stop for a bite before heading back to Adeje.

PRACTICALITIES

Although you can do the walk easily enough in a pair of trainers, it is better to wear sturdy hiking boots. Bring drinking water (and perhaps a little food). It is now forbidden to swim in the stream or shower under the waterfall. To prevent overcrowding a daily limit of 200 visitors has been imposed. Entry costs €3 per person. To reserve a place, tel: 922/782-885.

Map of El Barranco del Infierno showing the trail from Adeje / Restaurante Otelo I, with numbered waypoints 1–5, La Cojedora Cascada, Cascada, and surrounding features: Barranco del Inglés, Estanque de la Atalaya, Lomo de las Layas, Barranco Chaxor, Tablero de Calderón 1073m, Roque de Abinque 1059m, Ifonche, 1015m, Roque Ajache 1034m, Montaña Carasco, Roque Negro 587m, Barranco del Infierno, Barranco del Agua, TF-1. Scale: 1 km / ½ mile.

2 THE NORTHEAST AND ANAGA MOUNTAINS

Tour

La Laguna makes a perfect starting point for exploring the wild range of the Anaga Mountains to the northeast. You can complete it in various ways, and the following circuit could just as easily start at Santa Cruz de Tenerife or San Andrés, which lie along the initial stage (the Chinamada option is a three-hour walk). Be prepared for spectacular scenery, some rural backwaters, and changeable weather.

DISTANCE 93km/57.5 miles **TIME** A day trip including 2–3 hours' driving time
START/END POINT La Laguna ✚ 181 D4

1–2

From **La Laguna** (▶ 70–72) take the TF5 motorway east to Santa Cruz de Tenerife and then continue north towards San Andrés (▶ 55–56). You might want to start your day with a swim at the lovely **Playa de las Teresitas** (▶ 56). Otherwise, plunge straight in by taking the TF12 mountain road that winds north away from San Andrés.

2–3

In the space of just 9km (5.5 miles) you climb about 600m (1,968 feet) along this twisting road. As you snake through the mountain contours, sweeping vistas of the coast come repeatedly into view. Take the turn-off to **Taganana** (▶ 73) – the TF134 road. Just before the Túnel del Bailadero is a parking area to the right, and a lookout point. On emerging from the tunnel the magnificent sight of the Atlantic is below. On your way down to Taganana there's a good viewpoint on the first hairpin bend. Northeast of Taganana rises the rock formation of the **Roque de las Ánimas**. It is worth stopping in Taganana, the Anaga range's main town, for a look around.

3–4

From Taganana the TF134 slips down to the coast and around the base of the Roque de las Ánimas (on the right). The first beach you reach is **Playa de San Roque**, popular with surfers and lined with several restaurants. This is the obvious place to stop for lunch, especially as in many of the small towns and

A village nestles above the Roque de las Ánimas along the rugged Anaga coast

kilometre (0.3 miles) to **Almáciga**, a nondescript hamlet that does, however, offer good views. The road ends at Benijo, which really feels like the end of the road. From here, you could walk along the northeast coast as far as the **Roque Bermejo** (▶ 75), about three hours away.

5–6

If you are driving, however, there is no choice but to turn back. On reaching the TF12 you proceed a short way west and then turn east (following the signs for Chamorga). You shortly reach the **Mirador del Bailadero**. If there is no mist, you will enjoy extensive views over the north coast and south to San Andrés.

6–7

From the *mirador* the narrow TF123 road twists and turns, in part through thick woods, to the isolated settlement of **Chamorga** (▶ 75). Sunk deep in its rural torpor, Chamorga consists of a chapel, a spattering of houses and a strong population of dragon trees. A walking trail winds down the gorge, the **Barranco de Roque Bermejo**.

4–5

A side road cuts back half a

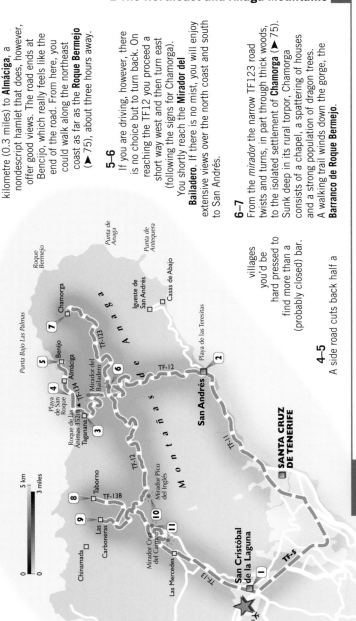

villages you'd be hard pressed to find more than a (probably closed) bar.

7–8

Again there is no choice but to backtrack. Follow the TF123 back for 12km (7.5 miles) to the junction with the TF12 and then continue west. About 7km (4.5 miles) west of the junction is the turn (the TF145) for Taborno and Las Carboneras. Make for **Taborno** (▶ 74), where the houses seem to be doing a balancing act on the back of a north–south ridge. From the northern half of the town are wonderful views of the mighty Anaga coast.

8–9

Backtracking from Taborno, you can turn right after 3km (2 miles) for **Las Carboneras** and then proceed from there on foot to **Chinamada** (▶ 74), or instead head about half a kilometre (0.3 miles) back towards the TF123 for the 5km (3-mile) walking trail to Chinamada, which, if you have the time, is more satisfying. Chinamada is curious, above all, for its houses built, in part, out of caves.

9–10

When you return to your car (if you decide to do one of the walks to Chinamada), head back to the TF123 and restart the westward journey. After about 2km (1 mile) the

Mirador Pico del Inglés is signposted south off the main road. From the lookout you have magnificent views over the south side of the Anaga mountain range and down to the coast around Santa Cruz de Tenerife.

10–11

A couple of kilometres further west you reach another fine lookout point on the south side of the main road, the **Mirador Cruz del Carmen**.

Apart from the views, there is a visitor centre for the Anaga natural reserve (daily 9:30–4). From the *mirador* you soon start to lose altitude as you exit the western extremity of the Anaga. The trip southwest along the TF12, and then the TF13 back to La Laguna via Las Mercedes is a brisker 9km (5.5 miles).

Magnificent vistas are repeated over and over while exploring the Anaga heights

3 THE NORTHWEST AND TENO MASSIF

Tour

Garachico, a charming coastal village with a handful of equally charming hotel options that are a far cry from the mass tourist ones to the south, makes a fine base for a driving tour. In the course of a day you can take in ocean views and wander a mountain village, see an ancient

DISTANCE 77km/48 miles **TIME** A day trip including about 1.5-2 hours' driving time
START/END POINT Garachico ✚ 176 C4

dragon tree, exotic butterflies and staggering cliff faces and finish off with seafood at sunset. Forest fires in July 2007 have temporarily scarred some of the mountainsides in this part of Tenerife, particularly around Masca. This will affect the views on this drive for the next four or five years.

1–2

It's a good idea to arrive in **Garachico** (▲ 98–99) the night before undertaking this excursion to give yourself time to relax. The natural rock pools, Castillo de San Miguel and especially the former Convento de San Francisco are all well worth some of your time. The following day, set off after an early breakfast for the 5km (3-mile) trip east to **Icod de los Vinos** (▲ 96–97). Here you can see the Drago Milenario, the oldest dragon tree on the island, estimated to be anything from 1,000 to 2,000 years old. The old town is worth a wander and you should consider a visit to the Mariposario del Drago (▲ 97), a butterfly zoo and museum full of exotic species.

2–3

From Icod take the TF820 road which heads west and rises slowly to **El Tanque** (9km/5.5

Garachico appears huddled in defence against volcanic fury

miles). As the road veers south it rises still more steeply, passing through Erjos and then reaching the **Puerto de Erjos** pass (1,117m/ 3,664 feet), 8km (5 miles) further on. You are now in the Teno Massif, which will remain a companion throughout the day. From the pass the road drops down for 4km (2.5 miles) to **Santiago del Teide**, a laid-back town.

3–4

A side road exits west from Santiago and quickly winds its way up into the massif to about 1,000m (3,280 feet). You soon reach a *mirador* with magnificent vistas out to sea. From this spectacular vantage point you drop into a series of tight, narrow switchbacks on the way to the delightful village of **Masca** (▶ 100–101), 5km (3 miles) from Santiago. You could spend an hour or so just wandering around the palm-filled village and any one of its restaurants make wonderful lunch stops. Perhaps try **Chez Arlette** (▶ 110). Virtually all of them have remarkable views.

4–5

From Masca go north, passing an impressive waterfall on the right and another huddle of houses belonging to the same municipality. Over the next 5km (3 miles) the road rises and

dips, then rises again to reach the exposed **Mirador de Baracán**. On a windy day it feels as though your car might take flight, so powerful are the ocean gusts.

5–6

Beyond the *mirador* the road winds north for 12km (7.5 miles) to **Buenavista del Norte** on the coast. In the high country here the land is largely barren except for hordes of cacti. Then come a couple of *pueblos*, like **Las Portelas** and **El Palmar**, which has given its name to a local wine, and scattered houses and small farm holdings. In the distance many of the farming terraces have become overgrown.

The rugged country of the northwest is one of the island's most beautiful attractions

right to Playa de las Arenas at the town exit. Veer left for Punta de Teno, but keep this fork in mind for the return trip.

Huge notices warn of rock falls and the danger of mudslides on this road – enter at your own risk. On a wet or very windy day you might think twice about proceeding, but otherwise plenty of people do it and the road itself is fine.

It gradually rises on an ever-higher shelf gouged out of the ominous dark volcanic cliff side. At the first tunnel there is a lookout point, although nowhere much to park. The most breathtaking moment arrives when you exit the second tunnel at the 5km (3-mile) mark. The sight of the sheer cliffs dropping, all jagged edges and deep shadows, into the ocean below, is humbling. For the next 4km (2.5 miles) the road slowly descends to line up with the low coast plain that opens up to your right. There six windmills stand still, generating nothing but curiosity. Along with the hill to your left, it

6–7
Proceed 9km (5.5 miles) west from Buenavista to the impressive **Punta de Teno** (▶ 106), along the TF445 road. Keep your eyes open for a turn-off

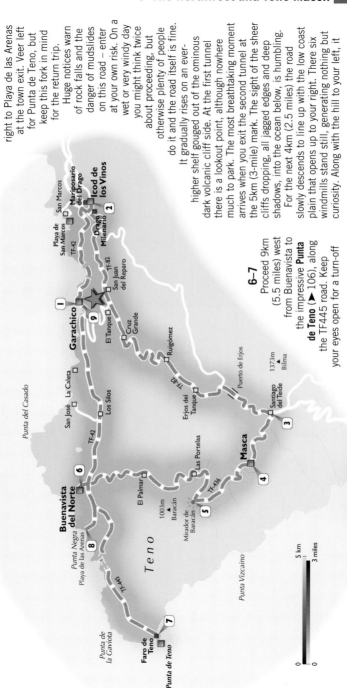

is covered with the peculiar shapes of the indigenous candelabra spurge bushes.

At the 9km (5.5-mile) mark, just short of the lighthouse, you reach the end of the road. Get out of the car to soak in the views of the majestic Teno coast to the south. From the lighthouse you can make out the islands of La Palma and La Gomera on a good day.

7–8
You now retrace your path towards **Buenavista**. Before you enter the town, look out for the Playa de las Arenas sign. Turn left and follow the signs for 2km (1 mile). You pass another fork with two other beaches signposted, Playa de las Mujeres (Women's Beach) and Playa del Fraile (Friar's Beach). Ignore them and keep on for **Playa de las Arenas.**

If the swell is up you won't see any sand, but if you have timed things right, you can sit down for a sunset drink at **Restaurante Burgado** (tel: 922/127-831) and perhaps stay for dinner. This simple place seems to have been carved from the coastal rock and a little cascade of water runs right through it.

8–9
Return to **Buenavista del Norte** and go east. The low-key urban spread means it is hard

to know when Buenavista del Norte finishes and Los Silos, 4km (2.5 miles) on, begins. You will notice that you are in serious banana country.

At **Los Silos** there is a modest black beach, which might be handy if you pass through earlier in the day. Otherwise continue on the 3km (2-mile) stretch to **Garachico.**

Just before you reach the town you pass the **Mirador del Emigrante.** Presumably it was so named because people could watch their emigrant friends and relatives sailing off to America.

Right: The Punta de Teno lighthouse is the end of the road

Page 167: Local folk groups gather at the start of the Fiesta Romería

Practicalities

BEFORE YOU GO

WHAT YOU NEED

		UK	Germany	USA	Canada	Australia	Ireland	Netherlands	Spain
● Required	Some countries require a passport to								
○ Suggested	remain valid for a minimum period								
▲ Not required	(usually at least six months) beyond								
△ Not applicable	the date of entry – check beforehand.								
Passport/National Identity Card		●	●	●	●	●	●	●	▲
Visa (regulations can change – check before you travel)		▲	▲	▲	▲	▲	▲	▲	▲
Onward or Return Ticket		●	●	●	●	●	●	●	●
Health Inoculations (tetanus and polio)		▲	▲	▲	▲	▲	▲	▲	▲
Health Documentation (➤ 172, Health)		●	●	▲	▲	▲	●	●	△
Travel insurance		●	●	●	●	●	●	●	●
Driving Licence (national)		●	●	●	●	●	●	●	●
Car Insurance Certificate		●	●	●	●	●	●	●	●
Car Registration Document		●	●	●	●	●	●	●	●

WHEN TO GO

Santa Cruz

Low season   High season

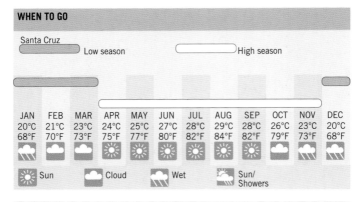

JAN	FEB	MAR	APR	MAY	JUN	JUL	AUG	SEP	OCT	NOV	DEC
20°C	21°C	23°C	24°C	25°C	27°C	28°C	29°C	28°C	26°C	23°C	20°C
68°F	70°F	73°F	75°F	77°F	80°F	82°F	84°F	82°F	79°F	73°F	68°F

☀ Sun   ☁ Cloud   🌧 Wet   🌦 Sun/ Showers

The temperatures above are the **average daily maximum** for each month. Although the Atlantic can be chilly, Tenerife is a year-round seaside destination. But the island's weather isn't uniform. The north coast and mountain areas are subtropical, while the south is arid and dry. Rainfall is at its highest in the north, where it can reach 750mm (30 inches) a year (but less than 20mm/0.75 inches in the southwest). Most rain falls from November to February. The upper reaches of Mount Teide are generally snow-capped in winter and well into spring. Even at the height of summer it can be very cold. In winter it can get cold elsewhere in the evening. High season for northern Europeans escaping winter is December to March, but Spaniards crowd in during summer. A beautiful time to come is in spring when the air is crisp and the flowers in full bloom.

GETTING ADVANCE INFORMATION

Websites

- Spanish Tourist Board: www.spain.info
- Tenerife Tourist Board: www.todotenerife.es

- Canary Islands Tourist Board: www.turismodecanarias.com
- www.etenerife.com is a useful unofficial website

In the UK

Spanish Tourist Office
PO Box 4009,
London W1A 6NB
☎ 020 7486 8077
www.tourspain.co.uk

GETTING THERE

By Air Tenerife absorbs a good percentage of the air traffic arriving in the Canary Islands. Most international and charter flights arrive in the modern **Tenerife Sur (Reina Sofia)** Airport in the south. Some international flights, along with a large share of Spanish mainland and inter-island flights, arrive at **Tenerife Norte (Los Rodeos)** Airport.

From the Islands **Binter Canarias** airlines runs daily flights from the Canary Islands, almost all of them to Tenerife Norte (Los Rodeos) Airport.

From the UK **Iberia** flies scheduled services from London to Tenerife via Madrid. However, there's a vast choice of direct flights through low-cost airlines including **Easyjet** and **Jet 2** plus hundreds of flights through holiday company airlines.

From the Rest of Europe **Iberia** flies to Tenerife from most European capitals via Barcelona or Madrid. Charter flights also operate from numerous cities across the continent.

From North America There are no direct flights from the USA or Canada, although you can fly with **Iberia** from New York, Los Angeles, Montreal and several other centres via Madrid. Iberia offers code-share with British Airways and American Airlines.

From Australia and New Zealand There are no direct flights to Spain but British Airways, Qantas and Cathy Pacific are One World alliance partners with Iberia for flights.

By Boat Regular inter-island car ferries and fast boats connect Santa Cruz with Las Palmas on Gran Canaria and Los Cristianos in southern Tenerife with the western islands (La Gomera, El Hierro and La Palma). A weekly ferry runs from Cádiz (on the Spanish mainland) to Tenerife – it takes almost two days.

TIME

Unlike the rest of Spain, the Canary Islands observe Greenwich Mean Time (GMT). Summer time (GMT+1) operates from the last Sunday in March to the last Sunday in October.

CURRENCY AND FOREIGN EXCHANGE

The euro (€) is the official currency of Spain. Euro notes are in denominations of 5, 10, 20, 50, 100, 200 and 500; coins come in denominations of 1, 2 and 5 bronze-coloured euro cents and 10, 20 and 50 gold-coloured euro cents. In addition there is a 1 euro coin with a silver centre and gold surround and a 2 euro coin with a gold centre and silver surround.

Credit and debit cards are widely accepted for purchases. **Traveller's cheques** are often accepted too, although generally you are better off exchanging them for cash.

Exchange Banks generally offer the best rates for changing foreign currency and travellers' cheques. Commissions and exchange rates can vary wildly. You will need to present your passport when changing cash or travellers' cheques. You can also use credit and debit cards (Visa and Mastercard are the most widely accepted) for cash advance in banks and from cash machines (ATMs). You will usually be charged by your bank for the service.

In the USA
Tourist Office of Spain
☎ 212/265-8822
www.okspain.org

In Canada
Tourist Office of Spain
2 Bloor Street West
Toronto, Ontario M4W 3E2
☎ (416) 961-3131
toronto@tourspain.es

For a complete list of Spanish tourist offices abroad, see www.spain.info

WHEN YOU ARE THERE

CLOTHING SIZES

UK	Rest of Europe	USA		
36	46	36		
38	48	38		
40	50	40		
42	52	42	Suits	
44	54	44		
46	56	46		
7	41	8		
7.5	42	8.5		
8.5	43	9.5		
9.5	44	10.5	Shoes	
10.5	45	11.5		
11	46	12		
14.5	37	14.5		
15	38	15		
15.5	39/40	15.5		
16	41	16	Shirts	
16.5	42	16.5		
17	43	17		
8	34	6		
10	36	8		
12	38	10		
14	40	12	Dresses	
16	42	14		
18	44	16		
4.5	38	6		
5	38	6.5		
5.5	39	7		
6	39	7.5	Shoes	
6.5	40	8		
7	41	8.5		

NATIONAL HOLIDAYS

1 Jan	New Year's Day
6 Jan	Epiphany
Feb/Mar	Carnaval Tuesday
Mar/Apr	Holy Thursday
Mar/Apr	Good Friday, Easter Monday
1 May	Labour Day
30 May	Canary Islands' Day
15 Aug	Feast of the Assumption
12 Oct	Spanish National Day
1 Nov	All Saints' Day
6 Dec	Constitution Day
8 Dec	Feast of the Immaculate Conception
25 Dec	Christmas Day

OPENING HOURS

○ Shops   ● Post Offices
● Offices   ● Museums
● Banks   ● Pharmacies

8am 9am 10am noon 1pm 2pm 4pm 5pm 7pm

□ Day   ▨ Midday   ▨ Evening

Offices Most government offices open Mon–Fri 9–2.
Shops Shops are generally open Mon–Fri 9–2 and 4:30/5–8. Many shops, travel agents and other businesses open on Sat. Big department stores such as the El Corte Inglés chain tend to open Mon–Sat 9–9.
Banks Banks are usually open Mon–Fri 8:30–2. Some open on Sat morning.
Post Offices Most post offices open Mon–Fri 8:30–2:30 and Sat 9:30–1. The main branch in Santa Cruz de Tenerife is open longer hours (▶ 171).
Museums Museums are sometimes closed for a period during lunch.

TIME DIFFERENCES

GMT	Tenerife	Mainland Spain	Germany	USA (NY)
12 noon	12 noon	1pm	1pm	7am

PERSONAL SAFETY

Violence against tourists is unusual. Theft from cars is the most common form of crime. To help prevent crime:
- Do not leave valuables on the beach or poolside.
- Always lock valuables in hotel safety deposit boxes.
- Never leave anything inside your car.
- Avoid walking alone at night.
- Do not carry around more cash than you need.

Police assistance:
☎ 112 from any phone

TELEPHONES

The blue and green public telephones take coins and phonecards (*tarjetas telefónicas*), which are available from post offices and *estancos* (tobacconists). A few also accept credit cards and have the appropriate sign. The cheap rate for international calls is 10pm–8am and all day Sunday.

International Dialling Codes
Dial 00 followed by

UK:	44
USA/Canada:	1
Ireland:	353
Australia:	61
Germany:	49

POST

Post boxes are yellow. The post office in **Santa Cruz de Tenerife** is at Plaza de España, open Mon–Fri 8:30am– 8:30pm, Sat 9:30am–1pm. Stamps *(sellos)* are available from post offices, hotels, news kiosks and tobacconists. It will take about a week for a postcard to get to the UK.

ELECTRICITY

The power supply is 220–225 volts. Sockets take standard continental-style plugs with two round pins. Visitors from the UK require an adaptor (often available at the airport) and visitors from the USA will require a voltage transformer.

TIPS/GRATUITIES

Tipping is not expected for all services, and rates are lower than in some countries. As a general guide:

Restaurants	up to 10%
Cafés/bars	Small change
Tour guides	€1
Taxis	Small change
Hairdressers	Small change
Chambermaids	€1
Porters	€1
Toilets	Small change

POLICE 112	
FIRE 112	
AMBULANCE 112	

HEALTH

 Insurance EU nationals can get free or reduced-rate emergency medical treatment with the relevant documentation (European Health Insurance Card for UK nationals) although private medical insurance is strongly recommended and is essential for all other visitors.

 Dental Services Dentists operate privately (see the Yellow Pages/*Páginas Amarillas*). Treatment may be covered by your insurance.

 Weather Visitors from cooler countries are especially vulnerable to the effects of the sun. You should cover up with a high-factor sunblock and drink plenty of non-alcoholic fluids. Children need to be well protected, especially when playing near the sea, as water and sand reflect the sun's rays.

 Drugs Prescription and non-prescription drugs and medicines are available from pharmacies, usually distinguished by a large green cross. Outside normal hours, a notice on the door of each pharmacy should give the address of the nearest duty chemist.

 Safe Water Tap water is generally safe to drink. Mineral water is widely available and inexpensive, especially when bought at supermarkets in large containers. If you see a sign *agua no potable* at a fountain, don't drink from it.

CONCESSIONS

Students Tenerife and the other Canary Islands do not attract backpacking youngsters in any great way. There are few concessions for students and holders of an International Student Identity Card aren't going to get much mileage out of it. Museums are generally free and it is not recognised for much else.

Senior Citizens Tenerife, which is geared up for tourists and has a benign climate, is a popular destination for older travellers. You can travel independently with ease or organise a package through tour operators specialising in holidays for senior citizens.

TRAVELLING WITH A DISABILITY

Although things are improving, many public buildings, hotels and restaurants remain inaccessible to wheelchair users. Some buses and taxis in Santa Cruz have been adapted for wheelchair access. For more information on what has been done to help visitors with disabilities see the Tourism for All website at www.tourismforall.org.uk.

CHILDREN

Hotels and restaurants are generally very child friendly, and many hotels have playgrounds, parks, mini-golf and children's pools. Some tour operators also provide children's clubs and activities as part of your holiday. However, baby-changing facilities are rare.

TOILETS

There are few public toilets so it's a good idea to make the most of visits to hotels, museums, restaurants, cafés, bars and shops.

CUSTOMS

The import of wildlife souvenirs sourced from rare or endangered species may be either illegal or require a special permit. Before buying, check your home country's customs regulations.

CONSULATES AND EMBASSIES

UK ☎ 922/286-863	**USA** ☎ 91 587 2200 (Madrid)	**Ireland** ☎ 928/297-728 (Gran Canaria)	**Australia** ☎ C91 353 6600 (Madrid)	**Canada** ☎ 91 423 3250 (Madrid)	

Spanish (*español*), also known as Castilian (*castellano*) to distinguish it from other tongues spoken in Spain, is the language of the Canary Islands. The islanders' version has a sing-song quality more reminiscent of the Spanish spoken in Latin America than the mainland.

GREETINGS AND COMMON WORDS

Do you speak English? **¿Habla inglés?**
I don't understand **No entiendo**
I don't speak Spanish **No hablo español**
Yes/No **Sí/no**
OK **Vale/de acuerdo**
Please **Por favor**
Thank you (very much) **(Muchas) gracias**
You're welcome **De nada**
Hello/Goodbye **Hola/adiós**
Good morning **Buenos días**
Good afternoon/evening **Buenas tardes**
Good night **Buenas noches**
How are you? **¿Qué tal?**
Excuse me **Perdón**
How much is this? **¿Cuánto vale?**
I'd like... **Quisiera/me gustaría**

EMERGENCY!

Help! **¡Socorro!/¡Ayuda!**
Could you help me please? **¿Podría ayudarme por favor?**
Could you call a doctor please? **¿Podría llamar a un médico por favor?**

NUMBERS

0	**cero**	20	**veinte**
1	**uno/una**	21	**veintiuno**
2	**dos**	30	**treinta**
3	**tres**	40	**cuarenta**
4	**cuatro**	50	**cincuenta**
5	**cinco**	60	**sesenta**
6	**seis**	70	**setenta**
7	**siete**	80	**ochenta**
8	**ocho**	90	**noventa**
9	**nueve**	100	**cien**
10	**diez**	101	**ciento uno**
11	**once**	110	**ciento diez**
12	**doce**	120	**ciento veinte**
13	**trece**	200	**doscientos/**
14	**catorce**		**cienta**
15	**quince**	500	**quinientos/**
16	**dieciséis**		**quinientas**
17	**diecisiete**	1000	**mil**
18	**dieciocho**	5000	**cinco mil**
19	**diecinueve**		

DIRECTIONS AND TRAVELLING

Aeroplane **Avión**
Airport **Aeropuerto**
Car **Coche**
Boat **Barco**
Bus **Autobús/guagua**
Bus stop **Parada de autobús**
Station **Estación**
Ticket (single/return) **Billete (de ida/de ida y vuelta)**
I'm lost **Me he perdido**
Where is…? **¿Dónde está...?**
How do I get to...? **¿Cómo llego a...?**
the beach **la playa**
the telephone **el teléfono**
the toilets **los servicios**
Left/right **Izquierda/derecha**
Straight on **Todo recto**

ACCOMMODATION

Do you have a single/double room available?
¿Tiene una habitación individual/doble?
with/without bath/toilet/shower
con/sin baño/lavabo/ducha
Does that include breakfast? **¿Incluye el desayuno?**
Could I see the room? **¿Puedo ver la habitación?**
I'll take this room **Cojo esta habitación**
One night **Una noche**
Key **Llave**
Lift **Ascensor**
Sea views **Vistas al mar**

DAYS

Today	**Hoy**
Tomorrow	**Mañana**
Yesterday	**Ayer**
Later	**Más tarde**
This week	**Esta semana**
Monday	**Lunes**
Tuesday	**Martes**
Wednesday	**Miércoles**
Thursday	**Jueves**
Friday	**Viernes**
Saturday	**Sábado**
Sunday	**Domingo**

RESTAURANT

I'd like to book a table
Quisiera reservar una mesa
A table for two please
Una mesa para dos, por favor
Could we see the menu, please?
¿Nos trae la carta, por favor?
What's this? **¿Qué es esto?**
A bottle/glass of…
Una botella/copa de…

Could I have the bill please?
¿La cuenta, por favor?
Service charge included
Servicio incluido
Waiter/waitress **Camarero/a**
Breakfast **Desayuno**
Lunch **Almuerzo**
Dinner **Cena**
Menu **La carta**

MENU READER

a la plancha grilled
aceite oil
aceituna olive
agua water
ajo garlic
almendra almond
anchoas anchovies
arroz rice
atún tuna

bacalao cod
berenjena aubergines
bistec steak
bocadillo sandwich

café coffee
calamares squid
cangrejo crab
carne meat
cebolla onion
cerdo pork
cerezas cherries
cerveza beer
champiñones mushrooms
chocolate chocolate
chorizo spicy sausage
chuleta chop
conejo rabbit
cordero lamb
crema cream
crudo raw
cubierto(s) cover (cutlery)
cuchara spoon
cuchillo knife
embutidos sausages
ensalada salad

entrante starter
espárragos asparagus

filete fillet
flan crème caramel
frambuesa raspberry
fresa strawberry
frito fried
fruta fruit

galleta biscuit
gambas prawns
gazpacho andaluz gazpacho (cold soup)
guisantes peas

habas broad beans
helado ice cream
hígado liver
huevos fritos/ revueltos fried/scrambled eggs

jamón serrano ham (cured)
jamón York ham (cooked)
judías beans
judías verdes French beans
jugo fruit juice

langosta lobster
leche milk
lechuga lettuce
legumbres pulses
lengua tongue
lenguado sole
limón lemon

lomo de cerdo pork tenderloin

mantequilla butter
manzana apple
mariscos seafood
mejillones mussels
melocotón peach
melón melon
merluza hake
mero sea bass
miel honey

naranja orange

ostra oyster

pan bread
papas arrugadas Canarian-style boiled potatoes
patata potato
patatas fritas chips
pato duck
pepinillo gherkin
pepino cucumber
pera pear
perejil parsley
pescado fish
pez espada swordfish
picante hot/spicy
pimientos red/ green peppers
piña pineapple
plátano banana
pollo chicken
postre dessert
primer plato first course
pulpo octopus

queso cheese

rape monkfish
relleno filled/stuffed
riñones kidneys

salchicha sausage
salchichón salami
salmón salmon
salmonete red mullet
salsa sauce
seco dry
segundo plato main course
solomillo de ternera fillet of beef
sopa soup

té tea
tenedor fork
ternera beef
tocino bacon
tortilla española Spanish omelette
tortilla francesa plain omelette
trucha trout

uva grape

verduras green vegetables
vino blanco/ rosado/tinto white/rosé/red wine

zanahorias carrots

San Cristóbal
de la Laguna

SANTA CRUZ DE
TENERIFE
■ 182/183

180/181

Puerto de
la Cruz

Garachico

Tenerife

176/177

Agulo

184/185

San Sebastián
de la Gomera

La Gomera

178/179

Playa de las Américas

Los Cristianos

To identify the regions, see the map on the inside of the front cover

Regional Maps

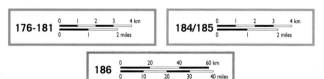

▬▬ Major route	▦ Built-up area
▭▭ Motorway	▫ Town/village
▭▭ Major road	◪ Featured place of interest
— Main road	▪ Place of interest
— Secondary road	✈ Airport
— River	☼ Viewpoint/mirador
⋯ Seasonal river	▲ Height in metres
▦ National Park	

176-181   0   1   2   3   4 km / 0   1   2 miles

184/185   0   1   2   3   4 km / 0   1   2 miles

186   0   20   40   60 km / 0   10   20   30   40 miles

Streetplan

▭▭ Dual road	◪ Featured place of interest
▭▭ Main road	𝒊 Tourist Information
▭▭ Other road	▦ Park
⋯ Minor road	▦ Important building
✝ Church	

182/183   0   50   100 metres / 0   50   100 yards

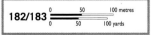

Atlas

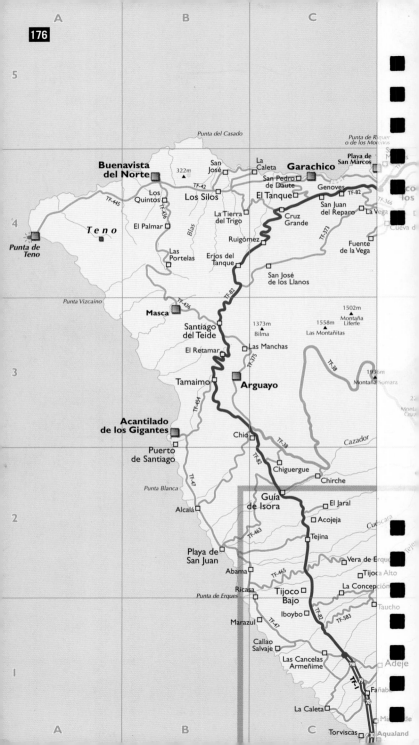

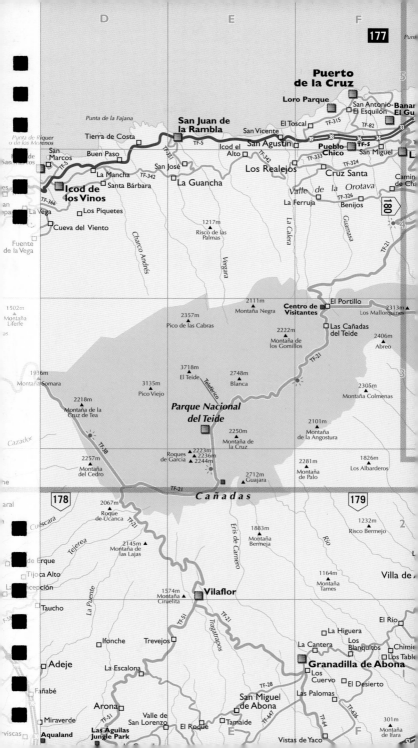

Punta de la Fajana

Puerto de la Cruz

Loro Parque

San Antonio-**Banar**
El Esquilón **El Gu**

El Toscal　TF-315

TF-82

Punta de Riquer
o de los Morenos

Punta de Riquer
o de los Morenos

Tierra de Costa

**San Juan de
la Rambla**

San Vicente

San Agustin

San Marcos

Buen Paso

Icod el
Alto

**Pueblo
Chico**

TF-5

San Miguel

San José

**Icod de
los Vinos**

La Mancha　TF-342

Santa Bárbara

La Guancha

Los Realejos

TF-342

TF-333

Cruz Santa

Camin
de Cha

TF-5

La Vega

Los Piquetes

La Ferruja

TF-326

Benijos

180

TF-21

Cueva del Viento

Fuente
de la Vega

Valle de la Orotava

La Galera

La Calera

Guamasa

1217m
Risco de las
Palmas

Charco Andrés

Vergara

1502m
Montaña
Liferfe

as

2111m
Montaña Negra

**Centro de
Visitantes**

El Portillo

2313m
Los Mallorquines

2357m
Pico de las Cabras

2222m
Montaña de
los Gomillos

**Las Cañadas
del Teide**

2406m
Abreo

1936m
Montaña Somara

3135m
Pico Viejo

3718m
El Teide

Teleférico

2748m
Blanca

TF-21

2305m
Montaña Colmenas

3

2218m
Montaña de la
Cruz de Tea

**Parque Nacional
del Teide**

2250m
Montaña de
la Cruz

2101m
Montaña
de la Angostura

Cazador

TF-58

Roques
de García

▲2223m
▲2236m
▲2244m

2712m
▲ Guajara

2281m
Montaña
de Palo

1826m
Los Albarderos

2257m
Montaña
del Cedro

178

2067m
Roque
de Ucanca

TF-21

_C a ñ a d a s_

179

2

Cuéscara

TF-51

2145m ▲
Montaña
de las Lajas

Eris de Carnero

1883m
Montaña
Bermeja

Río

1232m
Risco Bermejo

de Erque

Tijoca Alto

Tejierea

La Puente

1574m
Montaña
Ciruelita ▲

Vilaflor

TF-21

1164m
Montaña
Tames

Villa de

cepción

Taucho

TF-51

Tragatrapos

El Río

Ifonche

Trevejos

La Higuera

La Cantera

Los
Blanquitos

Chimi

Los Table

Adeje

La Escalona

Los
Cuervo

Granadilla de Abona

El Desierto

Fañabé

Arona

Valle de
San Lorenzo

TF-28

Las Palomas

TF-64

TF-636

Miraverde

Aqualand

**Las Águilas
Jungle Park**

El Roque

Tamaide

TF-447

**San Miguel
de Abona**

E

Vistas de Yaco

301m
Montaña
de Ifara

F

-viscas

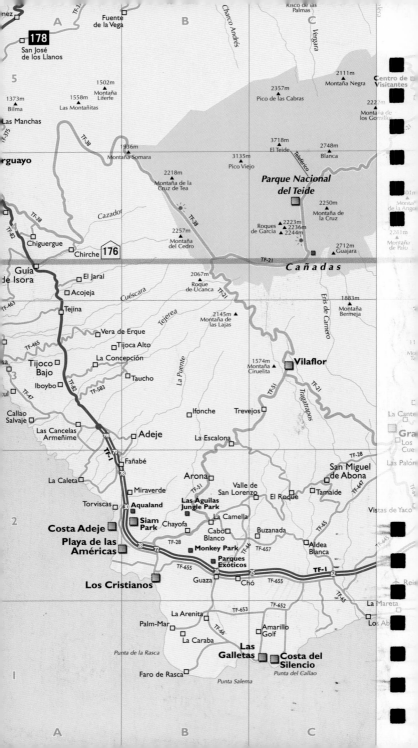

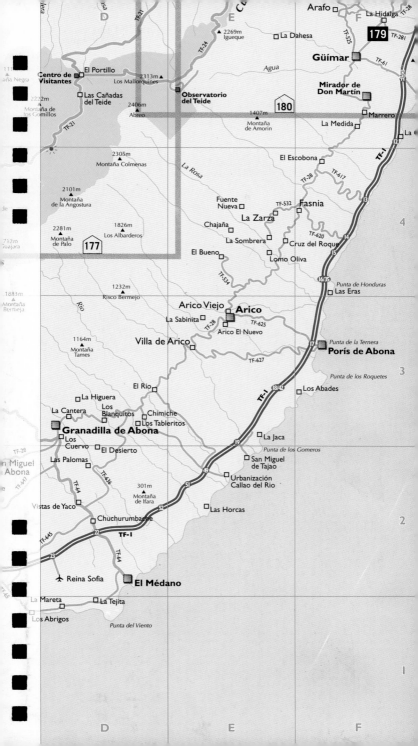

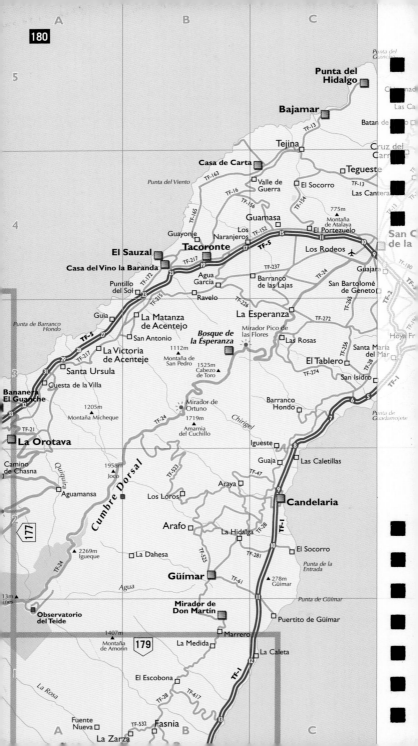

Punta del Hidalgo

Bajamar

Tejina

TF-13

Casa de Carta

Punta del Viento

TF-163

Valle de Guerra

El Socorro

Teguesto

TF-16

TF-156

TF-13

Las Cantoras

TF-154

Guamasa

775m
Montaña
de Atalaya

El Portezuelo

San C
de la

Guayonje

Los
Naranjeros

TF-152

15

Los Rodeos

10

TF-165

TF-101

Tacoronte

TF-5

Guajara

TF-180

El Sauzal

TF-217

21

TF-5

17

TF-237

TF-24

San Bartolomé
de Geneto

TF-2

Casa del Vino la Baranda

TF-172

Agua
García

Barranco
de las Lajas

Hoya Fr

Puntillo
del Sol

TF-215

21

Ravelo

TF-226

La Esperanza

TF-272

TF-265

Punta de Barranco
Hondo

Guía

TF-5

La Matanza
de Acentejo

Las Rosas

TF-256

Santa María
del Mar

TF-217

San Antonio

Bosque de
la Esperanza

Mirador Pico de
las Flores

TF-28

La Victoria
de Acenteje

1112m
Montaña de
San Pedro

El Tablero

Santa Ursula

1525m
Cabezo
de Toro

TF-274

San Isidro

TF-1

Cuesta de la Villa

Bananera
El Guanche

1205m
Montaña Micheque

Mirador de
Ortuno

Barranco
Hondo

6   5

Punta de
Guadamojete

TF-21

1719m
Amarnia
del Cuchillo

Chirigel

La Orotava

TF-24

Igueste

8

Camino
de Chasna

Guaja

Las Caletillas

1958m
Joco

TF-523

TF-47

9

Aguamansa

Los Loros

Araya

Candelaria

Quiquira

Cumbre Dorsal

Arafo

La Hidalga

TF-28

TF-1

10

2269m
Igueque

La Dahesa

TF-525

TF-281

El Socorro

La Rosa

Agua

Güimar

TF-61

278m
Güimar

Punta de la
Entrada

13m
ines

Observatorio
del Teide

Mirador de
Don Martin

Punta de Güimar

Puertito de Güimar

1407m
Montaña de Amorin

Marrero

La Medida

La Caleta

El Escobona

TF-1

La Rosa

TF-28

TF-617

Fuente
Nueva

TF-532

Fasnia

La Zarza

Punta Bajo Las Palmas

Punta del Cuincho
Punta de Tamadite
Roque Bermejo

del lgo

Chinamada

Almáciga
Playa de San Roque
Benijo
Chamorga

Taborno

Las Casas de Afur

Taganana
Lomo de las Bodegas

Las Carboneras

TF-138

Mirador del Bailadero
TF-134

TF-123

Punta de Anaga

tan de Abajo
Rio
Roque Negro
934m
A n a g a
735m

Cruz del Carmen
TF-143
TF-45
Pico del Inglés
TF-12
M o n t a ñ a s   d e   P i e d r a   G r a n d e
Viña Vieja
Igueste de San Andrés
Punta de Antequera

Tegueste
TF-12
732m Termino
Valle Brosque
Casas de Abajo

Las Mercedes
TF-113
692m
TF-12
TF-121

Las Canteras
TF-13
TF-113
Valle Vega
Maria Jiménez
TF-11
Playa de las Teresitas

ña lava uelo

San Cristóbal de la Laguna
Bufadero
San Andrés

Guajara
TF-180
TF-111
TF-111

Bartolomé de Geneto
TF-265
TF-5
TF-2
5
TF-94
4
3
2
TF-4
Parque Marítimo

SANTA CRUZ DE TENERIFE

Hoya Fría
TF-29
3

Santa María del Mar
TF-28
4

San Isidro
TF-1

Punta de Guadamojete

D   E   F

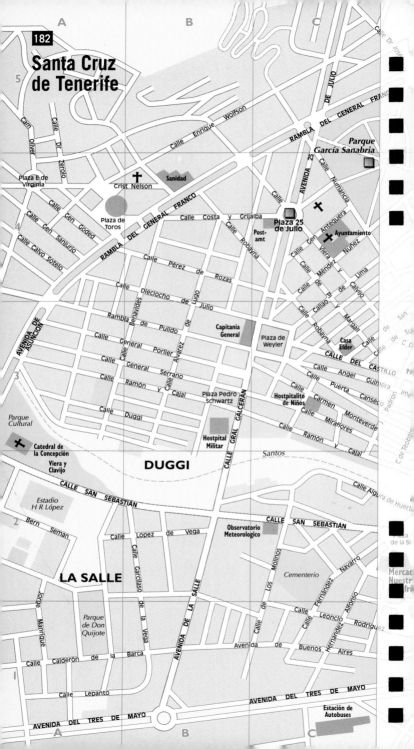

Santa Cruz de Tenerife

182

5

Calle Dr José

Calle Dr Zerolo

Cam Oliver

Calle Enrique Wolfson

RAMBLA DEL GENERAL FRANCO

AVENIDA 25 DE JULIO

Parque García Sanabria

Plaza E de Virginia

Calle Gen Coded

Calle Gen Sanjurio

Calle Calvo Sotelo

✝ Crist Nelson

Sanidad

Plaza de Toros

RAMBLA DEL GENERAL FRANCO

Calle Costa y Grijalba

Calle Robayna

Postamt

Plaza 25 de Julio

Calle Numancia

✝

Calle Gen Antequera

✝ **Ayuntamiento**

Calle Viera y Núñez

Calle Méndez y Lima

Calle de Po y Calvo

Calle Callao

Calle Margall

Calle de San

4

Calle Pérez de Rozas

Calle Dieciocho de Julio

Rambla de Pulido

Calle Benavides

Calle de Lugo

Calle de Robayna

Casa Elder

CALLE DEL CASTILLO

Calle de Su

Calle de C.C.

AVENIDA DE ASUNCIÓN

Calle General Porlier

Calle General Serrano

Calle de Álvarez

Capitanía General

Plaza de Weyler

Calle Angel Guimerá

Calle Puerta Canseco

Calle Ime

Padrón

C de Teobaldo

3

Calle Ramón y Cajal

Calle Duggi

Plaza Pedro Schwartz

CALLE GRAL GALCERÁN

Hospitalito de Niños

Calle Carmen

Calle Miraflores

Calle Monteverde

Parque Cultural

✝ **Catedral de la Concepción**

Viera y Clavijo

Hospital Militar

Calle Ramón y Cajal

DUGGI

Santos

Calle Algura de Huert

CALLE SAN SEBASTIÁN

Estadio H R López

Bern Seman

Calle Lopez de Vega

Calle Garcilaso de la Vega

Observatorio Meteorologico

CALLE SAN SEBASTIÁN

Calle de los Molinos

Cementerio

Calle Navarro

de la Si

Mercac Nuestr fri

2

LA SALLE

AVENIDA DE LA SALLE

Calle Jorge Manrique

Parque de Don Quijote

Calle Fernández

Calle Leoncio Rodríguez

Calle Hernández

Alfonso

1

Calle Calderón de la Barca

Avenida de Buenos Aires

Calle Lepanto

AVENIDA DEL TRES DE MAYO

AVENIDA DEL TRES DE MAYO

Estación de Autobuses

A

B

C

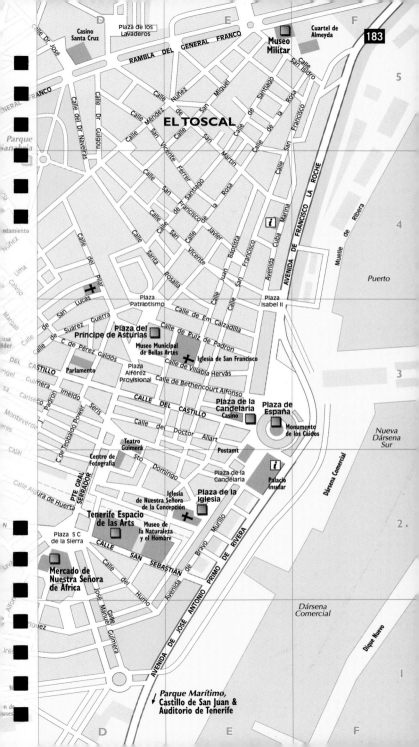

La Gomera

A   **B**   **C**

5

Los Órganos
Playa del Remo
Punta de los Órganos

Punta Sardina

4

Punta del Peligro

Arguamul
Valle Abajo
Tamargada
Vallehermoso
Las Rosas
Tazo
Rosa de las Piedras
Epina
Macayo
Alojera
Banda de las Rosas

Ag

TF-712

TF-711

Centr de Vis

Hermi

Las Casas
El Estanquillo
El Cedre

Taguluche
Arure
1136
Quemado
Parque Nacional de Garajonay
Mirador Ermita del Santo
Las Hayas
La Laguna Grande
Mirador César Manrique
Lomo del Balo
El Cercado
Chipude
Temocodá
1487
Garajonay
Igualero
Los Granados
El Hornillo
Valle Gran Rey
Gerian
1241
Fortaleza
La Calera
Benchijigua
Borbalán
Vueltas

Vegaipala

TF-713

3

Ermita de San Lorenzo
Imada

Las Salinas
Alajeró
Las Toscas

La Dama
Arguayoda
Quise

La Rajita

Punta de la Nariz
Cala Cantera
Punta Falcones
Caleta de la Jarrita
Punta del Becerro
La Gomera
Playa de la Salva
Faro Punta del Becerro

P Sa

2

1

A   **B**   **C**

5

4

Laja del Infierno

Agulo

Lepe

TF-711

Playa de Hermigua

Santa Catalina

Playa de la Caleta

Centro de Visitantes

Llano Campos

Hermigua

Las Nuevitas

Las Casas

El Curato

El Estanquillo

Parque Nacional de Majona

Punta Majona

1065 ▲ Encherada

Punta Gaviota

El Cedro

1062 ▲ Alto de Encherada

Punta Llana

TF-711

Ermita Nuestra Señora de Lourdes

Ermita de Nuestro Señora de Guadelupe

3

Chejelipes

El Molinito

Punta de Avalo

Mirador Degollada de Peraza

Casas de Langrero

Vegaipala

1083 ▲ Montaña de Destene

TF-713

Torre del Conde

San Sebastián de la Gomera

Seima

Playa del Cabrito

Las Toscas

Tejiade

Punta Gorda

2

La Gomera

Laguna de Santiago

Punta Gaviota

Playa la Salvajita

Playa de Santiago

Becerro

1

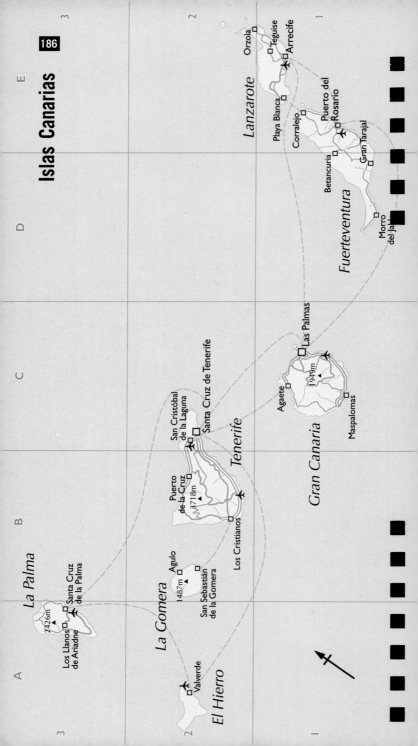

Islas Canarias

186

Picture Credits/Acknowledgements

The Automobile Association wishes to thank the following photographers, libraries and museums for their assistance with the preparation of this book.

Abbreviations for the pictures credits are as follows – (t) top; (b) bottom; (c) centre; (l) left; (r) right; (AA) AA World Travel Library.

5l Turismo de Tenerife; **5bl** AA/P Bennett; **5br** AA/C Jones; **6/7** Cubo Images/Robert Harding; **9** Juan Medina/Reuters/Corbis; **10** AA/R Moore; **11** AA/R Moore; **12** Jerónimo Alba/Alamy; **13** JoeFoxTenerife/Alamy; **14** Turismo de Tenerife; **15** Turismo de Tenerife; **16** Mary Evans Picture Library; **17** The Art Archive/Harper Collins Publishers; **18** AA/C Sawyer; **19** Turismo de Tenerife; **20/21** Stephen Frink Collection/Alamy; **22/23** Turismo de Tenerife; **24** AA/C Jones; **25** Turismo de Tenerife; **26/27** AA/C Jones; **28** AA/C Sawyer; **29l** AA/C Jones; **29bl** AA/R Moore; **29br** AA/C Jones; **43l** AA/C Jones; **43bl** AA/C Jones; **43br** AA/C Jones; **44** Turismo de Tenerife; **46** Turismo de Tenerife; **47** AA/C Jones; **48** Hemis/Alamy; **49t** AA/J Tims; **49b** AA/R Moore; **50** AA/C Jones; **51** AA/C Jones; **52** AA/R Moore; **53** AA/C Jones; **54** AA/C Sawyer; **55** AA/C Jones; **56** Turismo de Tenerife; **57** AA/J Tims; **58t** AA/J Tims; **58b** AA/R Moore; **59** AA/C Sawyer; **65l** AA/J Tims; **65bl** AA/C Jones; **65br** AA/J Tims; **66** AA/C Jones; **67t** AA/C Jones; 67b AA/C Jones; **68** AA/J Tims; **69t** AA/C Jones; **69b** Turismo de Tenerife; **70** AA/C Jones; **71** AA/C Jones; **72** AA/C Jones; **73** AA/J Tims; **74** AA/C Sawyer; **75** AA/C Jones; **76** AA/C Jones; **77** AA/J Tims; **78** AA/C Jones; **83l** Turismo de Tenerife; **83bl** AA/N Setchfield; **83br** AA/J Tims; **84** AA/C Jones; **85** AA/C Jones; **86** AA/K Paterson; **87t** AA/C Jones; **87b** AA/C Jones; **88/89** Rainer Jahns/Alamy; **89t** AA/C Jones; **90** AA/J Tims; **91** AA/C Jones; **92** AA/C Jones; **93** AA/C Sawyer; **94** Turismo de Tenerife; **95** AA/C Jones; **96** AA/C Sawyer; **97** AA/C Jones; **98** AA/C Jones; **99** AA/C Jones; **100** World Pictures/Photoshot; **101** LOOK Die Bildagentur der Fotografen GmbH/Alamy; **102** AA/R Moore; **103** Sergio Pitamitz/Robert Harding; **104** Turismo de Tenerife; **105** AA/C Jones; **106** AA/C Jones; **113l** AA/C Jones; **113bl** AA/C Jones; **113br** Turismo de Tenerife; **115t** AA/J Tims; **115b** AA/J Tims; **116** AA/C Sawyer; **117** AA/C Jones; **118/119** AA/R Moore; **120** AA/C Jones; **121** AA/R Moore; **122** AA/C Sawyer; **123** AA/C Sawyer; **124** AA/C Jones; **125t** AA/R Moore; **126** AA/C Jones; **127** AA/C Jones; **128** AA/C Sawyer; **129** AA/R Moore; **130** Turismo de Tenerife; **131** AA/C Sawyer; **132** AA/C Jones; **139l** AA/C Jones; **139bl** AA/C Jones; **139br** AA/C Jones; **140** AA/C Jones; **141t** AA/C Jones; **141b** AA/C Sawyer; **142** AA/C Sawyer; **143t** La Gomera Tourist Board; **143b** AA/L K Stow; **144** AA/C Jones; **145** AA/C Sawyer; **146** AA/C Sawyer; **147** AA/C Jones; **148** AA/C Sawyer; **149** AA/C Sawyer; **150** AA/C Sawyer; **151** AA/C Jones; **152** AA/C Jones; **157l** AA/C Jones; **157bl** AA/R Moore; **157br** AA/C Jones; **158** AA/J Tims; **160** AA/C Jones; **162** AA/C Jones; **163** AA/R Moore; **164** AA/C Sawyer; **166** AA/C Jones; **167l** AA/R Moore; **167bl** AA/R Moore; **167br** AA/J Tims; **171t** AA/C Jones; **171bl** AA/J Tims; **171br** AA/J Tims.

Every effort has been made to trace the copyright holders, and we apologise in advance for any accidental errors. We would be happy to apply any corrections in the following edition of this publication.

SPIRALGUIDE
Questionnaire

Dear Traveller

Your comments, opinions and recommendations are very important to us. Please help us to improve our travel guides by taking a few minutes to complete this simple questionnaire.

You do not need a stamp (unless posted outside the UK). If you do not want to remove this page from your guide, then photocopy it or write your answers on a plain sheet of paper.

Send to: The Editor, Spiral Guides, AA World Travel Guides, FREEPOST SCE 4598, Basingstoke RG21 4GY.

Your recommendations...
We always encourage readers' recommendations for restaurants, night-life or shopping – if your recommendation is used in the next edition of the guide, we will send you a FREE AA Spiral Guide of your choice. Please state below the establishment name, location and your reasons for recommending it.

_____

_____

_____

_____

_____

Please send me AA Spiral _____
(see list of titles inside the back cover)

About this guide...
Which title did you buy?

_____ **AA Spiral**

Where did you buy it?_____

When? m m / y y

Why did you choose an AA Spiral Guide? _____

_____

_____

_____

Did this guide meet your expectations?

Exceeded ☐   Met all ☐   Met most ☐   Fell below ☐

Please give your reasons_____

_____

_____

_____

_____

continued on next page...

Were there any aspects of this guide that you particularly liked?

_____

_____

_____

_____

_____

Is there anything we could have done better?

_____

_____

_____

_____

About you...

Name (Mr/Mrs/Ms) _____

Address _____

_____ **Postcode** _____

Daytime tel no _____ **email** _____

Please _only_ give us your email address and mobile phone number if you wish to hear from us about other products and services from the AA and partners by email or text or mms.

Which age group are you in?

Under 25 ☐   25–34 ☐   35–44 ☐   45–54 ☐   55–64 ☐   65+ ☐

How many trips do you make a year?

Less than one ☐   One ☐   Two ☐   Three or more ☐

Are you an AA member? Yes ☐   **No** ☐

About your trip...

When did you book? m m / y y   **When did you travel?** m m / y y

How long did you stay? _____

Was it for business or leisure? _____

Did you buy any other travel guides for your trip? ☐ Yes ☐ No

If yes, which ones? _____

_____

Thank you for taking the time to complete this questionnaire. Please send it to us as soon as possible, and remember, you do not need a stamp (unless posted outside the UK).